GW00585120

CONTENTS

TIPS ON USING AN AIR FRYING OVEN

Are you excited to bring variety to the table by using the air frying feature on your new Frigidaire appliance? Enjoy these helpful tips on how to get the most from your air fryer oven.

What foods can be cooked in an air fryer oven?

You can use the air fry setting on your oven for most foods that can traditionally be deep-fried. Some of our favorite recipes include:

- Chicken wings, chicken nuggets or pizza bites
- French fries, onion rings or sweet potato fries
- Brussel sprouts, kale, or zucchini fries

Can you cook battered food in an air fryer oven?

Crispy food needs enough oil to bind batters and coatings, but not too much or you'll end up with soggy results. If the food has a crumbly or floury outside texture, try spraying it with a little bit more oil.

If you're making air fried food from scratch, spray your homemade items with a light coating of oil (too much and the food won't get crispy) and arrange foods so the hot air circulates around each piece as much as possible.

Can you use olive oil while air frying?

Using cooking oils that can stand up to high temperatures is key while air frying, so avocado, grapeseed, and peanut oil are great for achieving crispy goodness. For best results, brush on lightly or spray an even coat of cooking spray made from these oils. Extra virgin olive oil is not an air fry-friendly oil due to its low smoke point, but extra light olive oil can be used for air frying because of its high smoke point. Other types of olive oil and some vegetable oils smoke at lower temperatures, meaning they will cause food to dry up quickly and prevent them from getting crispy.

Can you use aluminum foil in an air fryer oven?

Air fry works best on dark pans because they get and stay hot very quickly. Shiny foil reflects heat off the bakeware, which may change your results. When cooking with the Air fry Tray, we suggest putting a baking sheet on a rack a couple of positions below your tray. You can line that sheet with foil or parchment (or both) to catch any drips or crumbs, but you should never put aluminum foil, liners, or bakeware on the oven bottom. Items in this location can cause issues with air circulation and direct heat in any oven. Always keep the bottom of the oven clear so the air can circulate properly.

How do I keep my air frying oven clean?

Before using the air fry feature, place a cookie or baking sheet a rack or two under the Air Fry Tray to catch crumbs or drips. This will keep the bottom of the oven clean and free of fallen bits that can burn or cause odors later. Remember, do not place pans directly on the oven bottom to keep heat circulating correctly.

How do I clean the Air Fry Tray?

The Air Fry Tray is dishwasher safe, but for optimal cleaning, we recommend washing it by hand. It's designed to hold foods that already have some oil on them, which should keep food from sticking.

How do I limit the amount of smoke when using the Air Fry Tray?

Air fry uses really hot air to cook food fast and make it crunchy. Although air fry uses hot air to cook, remember that you are still frying your food so that it gets crispy! When some high-fat or greasy foods (like fresh wings) meet that hot air inside an oven, some smoke is normal. **If air fry is making a lot of smoke, try these tips:**

- When using the Air Fry Tray, put a baking sheet on a rack or two below the Air Fry Tray. This keeps drips and crumbs from landing on the oven bottom, where they can burn and create smoke. For additional protection, place some foil-lined parchment paper on the baking sheet. Parchment paper traps oil and keeps it from smoking.
- Use cooking oils that can stand up to high temperatures like avocado, grapeseed, and peanut oils. Cooking sprays made from these oils are available at the grocery store.
- Keep foil, parchment paper, and bakeware off the bottom of the oven. The oven bottom needs to stay clear so air can circulate.

- Don't overcrowd the food on your baking sheet or on the Air Fry Tray. If air can't circulate around each item, the cooking and crisping process may slow down and allow more grease to settle or drip.
- If your catch-tray is smoking, try placing parchment paper on it to hold grease. For extra-moist foods, you may have to use more. It's worth it!
- Some foods, like fresh wings and some vegetables, have a lot of moisture and may drip more than you expect. For items that might drip, use a pan with low sides if you're not using an Air Fry Tray.
- Air fry uses super-heated air, so if your oven bottom already has drips or crumbs on it (it happens!), those can smoke. Keep your oven bottom clean.
- If you have an oven vent, use it when cooking with air fry, like you would when using the cooktop.

BEEF PORK AND LAMB

Classic Pepperoni Pizza

Servings: 4
Cooking Time: 11 Minutes

Ingredients:

- Oil spray (hand-pumped)
- 1 pound premade pizza dough, or your favorite recipe
- ½ cup store-bought pizza sauce
- ¼ cup grated Parmesan cheese
- ¾ cup shredded mozzarella
- 10 to 12 slices pepperoni
- 2 tablespoons chopped fresh basil
- Pinch red pepper flakes

Directions:

1. Preheat the toaster oven to 425°F on BAKE for 5 minutes.
2. Spray the baking tray with the oil and spread the pizza dough with your fingertips so that it covers the tray. Prick the dough with a fork.
3. In position 2, bake for 8 minutes until the crust is lightly golden.
4. Take the crust out and spread with the pizza sauce, leaving a ½-inch border around the edge. Sprinkle with Parmesan and mozzarella cheeses and arrange the pepperoni on the pizza.
5. Bake for 3 minutes until the cheese is melted and bubbly.
6. Top with the basil and red pepper flakes and serve.

Traditional Pot Roast

Servings: 6
Cooking Time: 75 Minutes

Ingredients:

- 2 tablespoons olive oil
- 1 teaspoon garlic powder
- 1 teaspoon fresh thyme, chopped
- ¼ teaspoon sea salt
- ¼ teaspoon freshly ground black pepper
- 1 (3-pound) beef rump roast

Directions:

1. Preheat the toaster oven to 350°F on CONVECTION BAKE for 5 minutes.
2. In a small bowl, stir the oil, garlic, thyme, salt, and pepper. Spread the mixture all over the beef.
3. Place the air-fryer basket in the baking tray and place the beef in the basket.
4. In position 1, bake for 1 hour and 15 minutes until browned and the internal temperature reaches 145°F for medium.
5. Let the roast rest 10 minutes and serve.

Meatloaf With Tangy Tomato Glaze

Servings: 6
Cooking Time: 50 Minutes

Ingredients:

- 1 pound ground beef
- ½ pound ground pork
- ½ pound ground veal (or turkey)
- 1 medium onion, diced
- 1 small clove of garlic, minced
- 2 egg yolks, lightly beaten
- ½ cup tomato ketchup
- 1 tablespoon Worcestershire sauce
- ½ cup plain breadcrumbs
- 2 teaspoons salt
- freshly ground black pepper
- ½ cup chopped fresh parsley, plus more for garnish
- 6 tablespoons ketchup
- 1 tablespoon balsamic vinegar
- 2 tablespoons brown sugar

Directions:

1. Combine the meats, onion, garlic, egg yolks, ketchup, Worcestershire sauce, breadcrumbs, salt, pepper and fresh parsley in a large bowl and mix well.
2. Preheat the toaster oven to 350°F and pour a little water into the bottom of the air fryer oven. (This will help prevent the grease that drips into the bottom drawer from burning and smoking.)
3. Transfer the meatloaf mixture to the air fryer oven, packing it down gently. Run a spatula around the meatloaf to create a space about ½-inch wide between the meat and the side of the air fryer oven.
4. Air-fry at 350°F for 20 minutes. Carefully invert the meatloaf onto a plate (remember to remove the pan from the air fryer oven so you don't pour all the grease out) and slide it back into the air fryer oven to turn it over. Re-shape the meatloaf with a spatula if necessary. Air-fry for another 20 minutes at 350°F.
5. Combine the ketchup, balsamic vinegar and brown sugar in a bowl and spread the mixture over the meatloaf. Air-fry for another 10 minutes, until an instant read thermometer inserted into the center of the meatloaf registers 160°F.
6. Allow the meatloaf to rest for a few more minutes and then transfer it to a serving platter using a spatula. Slice the meatloaf, sprinkle a little chopped parsley on top if desired, and serve.

Seasoned Boneless Pork Sirloin Chops

Servings: 2
Cooking Time: 16 Minutes

Ingredients:

- Seasoning mixture:
- ½ teaspoon ground cumin
- ¼ teaspoon turmeric
- Pinch of ground cardamom
- Pinch of grated nutmeg
- 1 teaspoon vegetable oil
- 1 teaspoon Pickapeppa sauce
- 2½- to ¾-pound boneless lean pork sirloin chops

Directions:

1. Combine the seasoning mixture ingredients in a small bowl and brush on both sides of the chops. Place the chops on the broiling rack with a pan underneath.
2. BROIL 8 minutes, remove the chops, turn, and brush with the mixture. Broil again for 8 minutes, or until the chops are done to your preference.

Easy Tex-mex Chimichangas

Servings: 2
Cooking Time: 8 Minutes

Ingredients:

- ¼ pound Thinly sliced deli roast beef, chopped
- ½ cup (about 2 ounces) Shredded Cheddar cheese or shredded Tex-Mex cheese blend
- ¼ cup Jarred salsa verde or salsa rojo
- ½ teaspoon Ground cumin
- ½ teaspoon Dried oregano
- 2 Burrito-size (12-inch) flour tortilla(s), not corn tortillas (gluten-free, if a concern)
- ⅔ cup Canned refried beans
- Vegetable oil spray

Directions:

1. Preheat the toaster oven to 375°F .
2. Stir the roast beef, cheese, salsa, cumin, and oregano in a bowl until well mixed.
3. Lay a tortilla on a clean, dry work surface. Spread ⅓ cup of the refried beans in the center lower third of the tortilla(s), leaving an inch on either side of the spread beans.
4. For one chimichanga, spread all of the roast beef mixture on top of the beans. For two, spread half of the roast beef mixture on each tortilla.
5. At either "end" of the filling mixture, fold the sides of the tortilla up and over the filling, partially covering it. Starting with the unfolded side of the tortilla just below the filling, roll the tortilla closed. Fold and roll the second filled tortilla, as necessary.
6. Coat the exterior of the tortilla(s) with vegetable oil spray. Set the chimichanga(s) seam side down in the air fryer oven, with at least ½ inch air space between them if you're working with two. Air-fry undisturbed for 8 minutes, or until the tortilla is lightly browned and crisp.
7. Use kitchen tongs to gently transfer the chimichanga(s) to a wire rack. Cool for at last 5 minutes or up to 20 minutes before serving.

Chicken Fried Steak

Servings: 4
Cooking Time: 15 Minutes

Ingredients:

- 2 eggs
- ½ cup buttermilk
- 1½ cups flour
- ¾ teaspoon salt
- ½ teaspoon pepper
- 1 pound beef cube steaks
- salt and pepper
- oil for misting or cooking spray

Directions:

1. Beat together eggs and buttermilk in a shallow dish.
2. In another shallow dish, stir together the flour, ½ teaspoon salt, and ¼ teaspoon pepper.
3. Season cube steaks with remaining salt and pepper to taste. Dip in flour, buttermilk egg wash, and then flour again.
4. Spray both sides of steaks with oil or cooking spray.
5. Cooking in 2 batches, place steaks in air fryer oven in single layer. Air-fry at 360°F for 10 minutes. Spray tops of steaks with oil and cook 5 minutes or until meat is well done.
6. Repeat to cook remaining steaks.

Mustard-herb Lamb Chops

Servings: 2
Cooking Time: 15 Minutes

Ingredients:

- 2 tablespoons Dijon mustard
- 1 teaspoon minced garlic
- ¼ cup bread crumbs
- 1 teaspoon dried Italian herbs
- Zest of 1 lemon
- 4 lamb loin chops (about 1 pound), room temperature
- Sea salt, for seasoning
- Freshly ground black pepper, for seasoning
- Oil spray (hand-pumped)

Directions:

1. Preheat the toaster oven to 425°F on CONVECTION BAKE for 5 minutes.
2. Line the baking tray with parchment or aluminum foil.
3. In a small bowl, stir the mustard and garlic until blended.
4. In another small bowl, stir the bread crumbs, herbs, and lemon zest until mixed.
5. Lightly season the lamb chops on both sides with salt and pepper. Brush the mustard mixture over a chop and dredge it in the bread crumb mixture to lightly bread the lamb. Set the lamb on the baking tray and repeat with the other chops.
6. Spray the chops lightly with the oil, and in position 2, bake for 15 minutes until browned and the internal temperature is 130°F for medium-rare.
7. Rest the lamb for 5 minutes, then serve.

Barbecue-style London Broil

Servings: 5
Cooking Time: 17 Minutes

Ingredients:

- ¾ teaspoon Mild smoked paprika
- ¾ teaspoon Dried oregano
- ¾ teaspoon Table salt
- ¾ teaspoon Ground black pepper
- ¼ teaspoon Garlic powder
- ¼ teaspoon Onion powder
- 1½ pounds Beef London broil (in one piece)
- Olive oil spray

Directions:

1. Preheat the toaster oven to 400°F.
2. Mix the smoked paprika, oregano, salt, pepper, garlic powder, and onion powder in a small bowl until uniform.
3. Pat and rub this mixture across all surfaces of the beef. Lightly coat the beef on all sides with olive oil spray.
4. When the machine is at temperature, lay the London broil flat in the air fryer oven and air-fry undisturbed for 8 minutes for the small batch, 10 minutes for the medium batch, or 12 minutes for the large batch for medium-rare, until an instant-read meat thermometer inserted into the center of the meat registers 130°F (not USDA-approved). Add 1, 2, or 3 minutes, respectively (based on the size of the cut) for medium, until an instant-read meat thermometer registers 135°F (not USDA-approved). Or add 3, 4, or 5 minutes respectively for medium, until an instant-read meat thermometer registers 145°F (USDA-approved).
5. Use kitchen tongs to transfer the London broil to a cutting board. Let the meat rest for 10 minutes. It needs a long time for the juices to be reincorporated into the meat's fibers. Carve it against the grain into very thin (less than ¼-inch-thick) slices to serve.

Slow Cooked Carnitas

Servings: 6
Cooking Time: 360 Minutes

Ingredients:

- 1 pork shoulder (5 pounds), bone-in
- 2½ teaspoons kosher salt
- 1½ teaspoons black pepper
- 1½ teaspoons ground cumin
- 1 teaspoon dried oregano
- ¼ teaspoon ground coriander
- 2 bay leaves
- 6 garlic cloves
- 1 small onion, quartered
- 1 cinnamon stick
- 1 full orange peel (no white)
- 2 oranges, juiced
- 1 lime, juiced

Directions:

1. Season the pork shoulder with salt, pepper, cumin, oregano, and coriander.
2. Place the seasoned pork shoulder in a large pot along with any seasoning that did not stick to the pork.
3. Add in the bay leaves, garlic cloves, onion, cinnamon stick, and orange peel.
4. Squeeze in the juice of two oranges and one lime and cover with foil.
5. Insert the wire rack at low position in the Air Fryer Toaster Oven, then place the pot on the rack.
6. Select the Slow Cook function and press Start/Pause.
7. Remove carefully when done, uncover, and remove the bone.
8. Shred the carnitas and use them in tacos, burritos, or any other way you please.

Steak With Herbed Butter

Servings: 2
Cooking Time: 16 Minutes

Ingredients:

- 4 tablespoons unsalted butter, softened
- 1 tablespoon minced flat-leaf (Italian) parsley
- 1 tablespoon chopped fresh chives
- 2 cloves garlic, minced
- 1 teaspoon Worcestershire sauce
- 2 beef strip steaks, cut about 1 ½ inches thick
- 1 tablespoon olive oil
- Kosher salt and freshly ground black pepper

Directions:

1. Combine the butter, parsley, chives, garlic, and Worcestershire sauce in a small bowl until well blended; set aside.
2. Preheat the toaster oven to broil.
3. Brush the steaks with olive oil and season with salt and pepper. Place the steak on the broiler rack set over the broiler pan. Place the pan in the toaster oven, positioning the steaks about 3 to 4 inches below the heating element. (Depending on your oven and the thickness of the steak, you may need to set the rack to the middle position.) Broil for 6 minutes, turn the steaks over, and broil for an additional 7 minutes. If necessary to reach the desired doneness, turn the steaks over again and broil for an additional 3 minutes or until you reach your desired doneness.
4. Spread the herb butter generously over the steaks. Allow the steaks to stand for 5 to 10 minutes before slicing and serving.

Steak Pinwheels With Pepper Slaw And Minneapolis Potato Salad

Servings: 4
Cooking Time: 16 Minutes

Ingredients:

- Brushing mixture:
- ½ cup cold strong brewed coffee
- 2 tablespoons molasses
- 1 tablespoon tomato paste
- 2 garlic cloves, minced
- 1 tablespoon olive oil
- Garlic powder
- 1 teaspoon butcher's pepper
- 1 pound lean, boneless beefsteak, flattened to ⅛-inch thickness with a meat mallet or rolling pin (place steak between 2 sheets of heavy-duty plastic wrap)

Directions:

1. Combine the brushing mixture ingredients in a small bowl and set aside.
2. Cut the steak into 2 × 3-inch strips, brush with the mixture, and roll up, securing the edges with toothpicks. Brush again with the mixture and place in an oiled or nonstick 8½ × 8½ × 2-inch square baking (cake) pan.
3. BROIL for 8 minutes, then turn with tongs, brush with the mixture again, and broil for another 8 minutes, or until browned.

Pork Cutlets With Almond-lemon Crust

Servings: 3

Cooking Time: 14 Minutes

Ingredients:

- ¾ cup Almond flour
- ¾ cup Plain dried bread crumbs (gluten-free, if a concern)
- 1½ teaspoons Finely grated lemon zest
- 1¼ teaspoons Table salt
- ¾ teaspoon Garlic powder
- ¾ teaspoon Dried oregano
- 1 Large egg white(s)
- 2 tablespoons Water
- 3 6-ounce center-cut boneless pork loin chops (about ¾ inch thick)
- Olive oil spray

Directions:

1. Preheat the toaster oven to 375°F .
2. Mix the almond flour, bread crumbs, lemon zest, salt, garlic powder, and dried oregano in a large bowl until well combined.
3. Whisk the egg white(s) and water in a shallow soup plate or small pie plate until uniform.
4. Dip a chop in the egg white mixture, turning it to coat all sides, even the ends. Let any excess egg white mixture slip back into the rest, then set it in the almond flour mixture. Turn it several times, pressing gently to coat it evenly. Generously coat the chop with olive oil spray, then set aside to dip and coat the remaining chop(s).
5. Set the chops in the air fryer oven with as much air space between them as possible. Air-fry undisturbed for 12 minutes, or until browned and crunchy. You may need to add 2 minutes to the cooking time if the machine is at 360°F.
6. Use kitchen tongs to transfer the chops to a wire rack. Cool for a few minutes before serving.

BREAKFAST

Goat Cheese Rosemary Crostini With Roasted Garlic + Tomatoes

Servings: 20
Cooking Time: 25 Minutes

Ingredients:

- 4 to 5 large cloves garlic, trimmed, not peeled
- 1 ½ tablespoons olive oil
- 2 cups grape tomatoes
- Kosher salt and freshly ground black pepper
- 1 teaspoon balsamic or red wine vinegar
- 4 ounces soft, creamy goat cheese, softened (about ½ cup)
- 1 tablespoon minced fresh rosemary leaves
- 1 baguette loaf, cut into ½-inch-thick slices
- Fresh rosemary leaves or minced flat-leaf (Italian) parsley, for garnish (optional)

Directions:

1. Preheat the toaster oven to 400°F.
2. Place the garlic on an 8- to 12-inch square of aluminum foil and bring up the edges to make a shallow bowl. Drizzle the garlic with ½ tablespoon olive oil. Bring the foil over the garlic and fold the edges to make a sealed packet. Place the packet on one side of a 12 x 12-inch baking pan. (Note: Be sure to make the aluminum foil packet compact and place it on the pan but positioned so it is not near the heating element.)
3. Place the tomatoes in a medium bowl. Drizzle with the remaining tablespoon of olive oil and season with salt and pepper. Pour the tomatoes into a single layer on the other end of the baking pan. Roast, uncovered, for 20 to 25 minutes or until the edges of the tomatoes begin to brown and they are tender.
4. Remove the tomatoes and garlic from the oven and let cool slightly. Spoon the roasted tomatoes, with any collected liquid, into a medium bowl. When the garlic is cool enough to handle, gently squeeze the garlic into a small bowl and discard the garlic peels. Use the back of a spoon to mash the garlic. Stir the roasted garlic and vinegar into the tomatoes. Season with salt and pepper; set aside.
5. Stir the goat cheese and rosemary in a small bowl. Season it generously with pepper. Blend until smooth; set aside.
6. Toast the slices of the baguette in the toaster oven.
7. Distribute the goat cheese mixture evenly over the toasted bread slices. Top with a teaspoon of the roasted tomato-garlic mixture. If desired, garnish with fresh rosemary.

Christmas Eggnog Bread

Servings: 6
Cooking Time: 18 Minutes

Ingredients:

- 1 cup flour, plus more for dusting
- ¼ cup sugar
- 1 teaspoon baking powder
- ¼ teaspoon salt
- ¼ teaspoon nutmeg
- ½ cup eggnog
- 1 egg yolk
- 1 tablespoon butter, plus 1 teaspoon, melted
- ¼ cup pecans
- ¼ cup chopped candied fruit (cherries, pineapple, or mixed fruits)
- cooking spray

Directions:

1. Preheat the toaster oven to 360°F.
2. In a medium bowl, stir together the flour, sugar, baking powder, salt, and nutmeg.
3. Add eggnog, egg yolk, and butter. Mix well but do not beat.
4. Stir in nuts and fruit.
5. Spray a 6 x 6-inch baking pan with cooking spray and dust with flour.
6. Spread batter into prepared pan and air-fry at 360°F for 18 minutes or until top is dark golden brown and bread starts to pull away from sides of pan.

Espresso Chip Muffins

Servings: 6
Cooking Time: 20 Minutes

Ingredients:

- 1 cup all-purpose flour
- 6 tablespoons packed dark brown sugar
- 1 ¼ teaspoons baking powder
- 1 teaspoon instant espresso coffee powder
- ¼ teaspoon table salt
- ¼ teaspoon ground cinnamon
- ½ cup whole milk
- ¼ cup unsalted butter, melted and cooled slightly
- 1 large egg
- ½ teaspoon pure vanilla extract
- ½ cup mini semisweet chocolate chips

Directions:

1. Preheat the toaster oven to 375°F. Grease a 6-cup muffin pan.
2. Whisk the flour, brown sugar, baking powder, espresso, salt, and cinnamon in a medium bowl. Combine the milk, butter, egg, and vanilla in a small bowl until blended. Make a well in the center of the flour mixture and add the milk mixture. Stir until just combined. Fold in the chocolate chips.
3. Spoon the batter evenly into the prepared muffin cups. Bake for 18 to 20 minutes, or until a wooden pick inserted into the center comes out clean. Cool on a wire rack for 5 minutes, then remove the muffins from the pan to finish cooling on a wire rack. Serve warm or at room temperature. Store in an airtight container.

Individual Overnight Omelets

Servings: 2
Cooking Time: 45 Minutes

Ingredients:

- 1 tablespoon unsalted butter, softened
- 2 slices hearty white sandwich bread
- 2 ounces cheddar cheese, shredded (½ cup)
- 3 large eggs
- ¾ cup whole milk
- 1 teaspoon minced fresh thyme or ¼ teaspoon dried
- ¼ teaspoon table salt
- ¼ teaspoon pepper

Directions:

1. Spray two 12-ounce ramekins with vegetable oil spray. Spread butter evenly over 1 side of bread slices, then cut into 1-inch pieces. Scatter half of bread evenly in prepared ramekins and sprinkle with half of cheddar. Repeat with remaining bread and cheese.
2. Whisk eggs, milk, thyme, salt, and pepper in bowl until well combined. Pour egg mixture evenly over bread and press lightly on bread to submerge. Wrap ramekins tightly with plastic wrap and refrigerate for at least 8 hours or up to 24 hours.
3. Adjust toaster oven rack to middle position and preheat the toaster oven to 350 degrees. Unwrap ramekins and place ramekins on small rimmed baking sheet. Bake until puffed and golden, 30 to 35 minutes, rotating sheet halfway through baking. Serve immediately.

Savory Salsa Cheese Rounds

Servings: 6
Cooking Time: 6 Minutes

Ingredients:

- 1 French baguette, cut to make 12
- 1-inch slices (rounds)
- ¼ cup olive oil
- 1 cup Tomato Salsa (recipe follows)
- ½ cup shredded low-fat mozzarella
- 2 tablespoons finely chopped fresh cilantro

Directions:

1. Brush both sides of each round with olive oil.
2. Spread one side of each slice with salsa and sprinkle each with mozzarella. Place the rounds in an oiled or nonstick 8½ × 8½ × 2-inch square baking (cake) pan.
3. BROIL for 6 minutes, or until the cheese is melted and the rounds are lightly browned. Garnish with the chopped cilantro and serve.

Lemon-blueberry Muffins

Servings: 6
Cooking Time: 60 Minutes

Ingredients:

- ¾ cup (5¼ ounces) sugar, divided
- 2 teaspoons grated lemon zest, divided
- 1¼ cups (6¼ ounces) all-purpose flour
- 2 teaspoons baking powder
- ¼ teaspoon table salt
- ¾ cup sour cream
- 3 tablespoons unsalted butter, melted, divided
- 1 large egg

- 3¾ ounces (¾ cup) frozen blueberriesDirections:
- Adjust toaster oven rack to middle position and preheat the toaster oven to 400 degrees. Generously spray 6-cup muffin tin, including top, with vegetable oil spray. Combine 2 tablespoons sugar and 1 teaspoon lemon zest in small bowl; set aside.
- Whisk flour, baking powder, and salt together in bowl. Whisk sour cream, 2 tablespoons melted butter, egg, remaining 10 tablespoons sugar, and remaining 1 teaspoon lemon zest together in large bowl.
- Using rubber spatula, fold flour mixture into sour cream mixture until just combined. Fold in blueberries until evenly distributed; do not overmix. Using greased ⅓-cup dry measuring cup or #12 portion scoop, divide batter equally among prepared muffin cups; evenly distribute any remaining batter between muffin cups. Brush batter with remaining 1 tablespoon melted butter and sprinkle with sugar-zest mixture (about 1 teaspoon per muffin cup).
- Bake until muffins are golden brown and toothpick inserted in center comes out with few crumbs attached, 22 to 27 minutes, rotating muffin tin halfway through baking. Let muffins cool in muffin tin on wire rack for 10 minutes. Transfer muffins to rack and let cool slightly. Serve warm or at room temperature.

Baked Macs

Servings: 2
Cooking Time: 30 Minutes

Ingredients:

- 2 tablespoons rolled oats
- 2 tablespoons applesauce
- 1 tablespoon honey
- 1 teaspoon ground cinnamon
- Pinch of ground allspice
- Pinch of salt
- 2 McIntosh apples, cored
- Maple Yogurt Sauce (recipe follows)

Directions:

1. Preheat the toaster oven to 375° F.
2. Mix together the oatmeal, applesauce, honey, and seasonings in a small bowl. Spoon the mixture into the cavities of the apples and place the apples in an oiled or nonstick 8½ × 8½ × 2-inch square baking (cake) pan.
3. BAKE the apples for 30 minutes, or until tender. Serve chilled or warm with Maple Yogurt Sauce.

Cherries Jubilee

Servings: 4
Cooking Time: 10 Minutes

Ingredients:

- 1 15-ounce can cherries, pitted and drained, with 2 tablespoons juice reserved
- 1 tablespoon orange juice
- 1 tablespoon sugar
- 1 tablespoon cornstarch
- ¼ cup warmed Kirsch or Cognac
- Vanilla yogurt or fat-free half-and-half

Directions:

1. Combine the reserved juice, orange juice, sugar, and cornstarch in a shallow baking pan, blending well.
2. BROIL for 5 minutes, or until the juice clarifies and thickens slightly. Add the cherries and heat, broiling for 5 minutes more and stirring to blend. Remove from the oven and transfer to a flameproof serving dish.
3. Spoon the Kirsch over the cherries and ignite. Top with vanilla yogurt or drizzle with warm fat-free half-and-half and serve.

Blueberry Muffins

Servings: 8
Cooking Time: 14 Minutes

Ingredients:

- 1⅓ cups flour
- ½ cup sugar
- 2 teaspoons baking powder
- ¼ teaspoon salt
- ⅓ cup canola oil
- 1 egg
- ½ cup milk
- ⅔ cup blueberries, fresh or frozen and thawed
- 8 foil muffin cups including paper liners

Directions:

1. Preheat the toaster oven to 330°F.
2. In a medium bowl, stir together flour, sugar, baking powder, and salt.
3. In a separate bowl, combine oil, egg, and milk and mix well.
4. Add egg mixture to dry ingredients and stir just until moistened.
5. Gently stir in blueberries.
6. Spoon batter evenly into muffin cups.
7. Place 4 muffin cups in air fryer oven and bake at 330°F for 14 minutes or until tops spring back when touched lightly.
8. Repeat previous step to cook remaining muffins.

Beef And Bean Quesadillas

Servings: 2
Cooking Time: 30 Minutes

Ingredients:

- Quesadilla filling:
- 1 8-ounce flank steak, trimmed and cut into thin ⅛ × 2-inch strips
- 1 jalapeño pepper, seeded and minced
- 2 plum tomatoes, chopped
- 1 small onion, cut into thin strips
- 1 bell pepper, seeded and cut into thin strips
- 2 garlic cloves, minced
- 1 15-ounce can black beans, rinsed and drained
- 2 tablespoons chopped fresh cilantro
- ½ cup reduced-fat Monterey Jack cheese
- 4 6-inch flour tortillas
- Low-fat or fat-free sour cream

Directions:

1. Combine the filling ingredients in an oiled or nonstick 8½ × 8½ × 2-inch square baking (cake) pan, mixing well to blend.
2. BROIL for 10 minutes, remove from the oven, and turn the pieces with tongs. Broil for 10 minutes, or until the pepper, onion, and beef are cooked and tender. Remove from the oven and transfer to a bowl. Add the beans and cilantro and mix well.
3. Spread one quarter of the tortilla mixture in the center of each tortilla. Sprinkle each tortilla with 2 tablespoons cheese. Roll up the edges and lay each, seam side down, in the pan.
4. BROIL for 10 minutes, or until the tortillas are lightly browned and the cheese is melted. Serve with sour cream.

Sesame Wafers

Servings: 4
Cooking Time: 6 Minutes

Ingredients:

- ½ cup sesame seeds
- 1 tablespoon unbleached flour
- 1 tablespoon margarine, at room temperature
- 1 teaspoon dark brown sugar

Directions:

1. Preheat the toaster oven to 400° F.
2. Combine the sesame seeds, flour, margarine, and sugar in a small bowl, mixing well. Sprinkle equal portions into 4 individual 1-cup-size ovenproof dishes and press to cover the bottom evenly.
3. BAKE for 6 minutes, or until lightly browned.

Homemade Biscuits

Servings: 12
Cooking Time: 28 Minutes

Ingredients:

- 1 1/2 cups milk
- 1 tablespoon white vinegar
- 4 cups all-purpose flour
- 1/4 cup sugar
- 1 tablespoon plus 1 1/2 teaspoons baking powder
- 1 teaspoon salt
- 1 cup unsalted butter, cut into pieces
- Sausage Gravy

Directions:

1. Preheat the toaster oven to 375°F. Line a cookie sheet with parchment paper.
2. In a small bowl, stir milk and vinegar until blended. Set aside.
3. In a large bowl, combine flour, sugar, baking powder and salt. Cut in butter with a fork or a pastry blender until coarse crumbs form. Stir in the milk mixture until moistened (dough will be slightly moist).
4. On a well floured surface, roll dough to 3/4-inch thickness. Cut with a 3-inch round cookie cutter and arrange 2-inches apart on cookie sheet. Repeat with remaining dough.
5. Bake 26 to 28 minutes or until lightly browned.
6. Serve with Sausage Gravy, if desired.

DESSERTS

Strawberry Blueberry Cobbler

Servings: 6
Cooking Time: 30 Minutes

Ingredients:

- Berry filling:
- 1 10-ounce package frozen blueberries, thawed, or 1½ cups fresh blueberries
- 1 10-ounce package frozen strawberries, thawed, or 1½ cups fresh strawberries
- ½ cup strawberry preserves
- ¼ cup unbleached flour
- 1 teaspoon lemon juice
- Topping:
- ¼ cup unbleached flour
- 2 tablespoons margarine
- 1 tablespoon fat-free half-and-half
- ½ teaspoon baking powder
- 1 tablespoon sugar

Directions:

1. Preheat the toaster oven to 400° F.
2. Combine the berry filling ingredients in a large bowl, mixing well. Transfer to an oiled or nonstick 8½ × 8½ × 2-inch square baking (cake) pan. Set aside.
3. Combine the topping ingredients in a small bowl, blending with a fork until the mixture is crumbly. Sprinkle the mixture evenly over the berries.
4. BAKE for 30 minutes, or until the top is lightly browned.

Chocolate Cupcakes With Salted Caramel Buttercream

Servings: 12
Cooking Time: 20 Minutes

Ingredients:

- Cake Ingredients
- 1 egg
- ½ cup vegetable oil
- ½ cup buttermilk
- ½ teaspoon vanilla extract
- 1 cup granulated sugar
- 1 cup all-purpose flour
- ¼ cup dark cocoa powder
- 1 teaspoon baking soda
- ½ teaspoon salt
- ½ teaspoon instant espresso powder
- ½ cup boiling water (205°-212°F)
- Buttercream Ingredients
- ½ cup unsalted butter, room temperature
- ⅓ cup caramel sauce, room temperature
- ½ teaspoon vanilla extract
- ½ teaspoon kosher salt
- 1 cup powdered sugar

Directions:

1. Whisk together the egg, vegetable oil, buttermilk, and vanilla extract in a bowl and set aside.
2. Sift together sugar, flour, cocoa powder, baking soda, salt, and instant espresso in a large mixing bowl.
3. Add the wet ingredients into the dry and mix until well combined.
4. Pour in the boiling water slowly while whisking vigorously until the batter is smooth.
5. Line the muffin pan with cupcake liners, then pour in the batter.
6. Preheat the toaster Oven to 350°F.
7. Place the cupcakes on the wire rack, then insert the rack at mid position in the preheated oven.
8. Select the Bake and Fan functions, adjust time to 20 minutes, and press Start/Pause.
9. Remove when done and allow cupcakes to cool on a wire rack for 2 hours.
10. Beat butter using a stand mixer on medium speed for 1 minute or until smooth and fluffy.
11. Beat in the caramel sauce, vanilla, and salt for 2 minutes or until well combined. You may need to scrape down the side of the bowl occasionally.
12. Add the powdered sugar slowly, beating on low speed until fully incorporated.
13. Beat the buttercream on medium speed for 2 minutes or until smooth and creamy.
14. Pipe the buttercream onto the cooled cupcake using a decorated tip.
15. Place the cakes in the fridge for 30 minutes before serving.

Chocolate Caramel Pecan Cupcakes

Servings: 6
Cooking Time: 20 Minutes

Ingredients:

- 6 tablespoons all-purpose flour
- 6 tablespoons unsweetened cocoa powder
- ¼ teaspoon baking soda
- ¼ teaspoon baking powder
- ⅛ teaspoon table salt
- 6 tablespoons unsalted butter, softened
- ½ cup granulated sugar
- 1 large egg
- ½ teaspoon pure vanilla extract
- ½ cup sour cream
- BUTTERCREAM FROSTING
- ¼ cup unsalted butter, softened
- 1 ¾ cups confectioners' sugar
- 2 to 3 tablespoons half-and-half or milk
- 1 teaspoon pure vanilla extract
- Caramel ice cream topping
- ¼ cup caramelized chopped pecans

Directions:

1. Preheat the toaster oven to 350°F. Line a 6-cup muffin pan with cupcake papers.
2. Whisk the flour, cocoa, baking soda, baking powder, and salt in a small bowl; set aside.
3. Beat the butter and granulated sugar in a large bowl with a handheld mixer at medium-high speed for 2 minutes, or until the mixture is light and creamy. Beat in the egg well. Beat in the vanilla.
4. On low speed, beat in the flour mixture in thirds, alternating with the sour cream, beginning and ending with the flour mixture. The batter will be thick.
5. Spoon the batter evenly into the prepared cupcake cups, filling each about three-quarters full. Bake for 18 to 20 minutes, or until a wooden pick inserted into the center comes out clean. Place on a wire rack and let cool completely.
6. Meanwhile, make the frosting: Beat the butter in a large bowl using a handheld mixer on medium-high speed until creamy. Gradually beat in the confectioners' sugar. Beat in 2 tablespoons of half-and-half and the vanilla. Beat in the remaining tablespoon of half-and-half, as needed, until the frosting is of desired consistency.
7. Frost each cooled cupcake. Drizzle the caramel topping in thin, decorative stripes over the frosting. Top with the caramelized pecans.

Sweet Potato Donut Holes

Servings: 18
Cooking Time: 4 Minutes

Ingredients:

- 1 cup flour
- ⅓ cup sugar
- ¼ teaspoon baking soda
- 1 teaspoon baking powder
- ⅛ teaspoon salt
- ½ cup cooked mashed purple sweet potatoes
- 1 egg, beaten
- 2 tablespoons butter, melted
- 1 teaspoon pure vanilla extract
- oil for misting or cooking spray

Directions:

1. Preheat the toaster oven to 390°F.
2. In a large bowl, stir together the flour, sugar, baking soda, baking powder, and salt.
3. In a separate bowl, combine the potatoes, egg, butter, and vanilla and mix well.
4. Add potato mixture to dry ingredients and stir into a soft dough.
5. Shape dough into 1½-inch balls. Mist lightly with oil or cooking spray.
6. Place 9 donut holes in air fryer oven, leaving a little space in between. Air-fry for 4 minutes, until done in center and lightly browned outside.
7. Repeat step 6 to cook remaining donut holes.

Dark Chocolate Peanut Butter S'mores

Servings: 4
Cooking Time: 6 Minutes

Ingredients:

- 4 graham cracker sheets
- 4 marshmallows
- 4 teaspoons chunky peanut butter
- 4 ounces dark chocolate
- ½ teaspoon ground cinnamon

Directions:

1. Preheat the toaster oven to 390°F. Break the graham crackers in half so you have 8 pieces.
2. Place 4 pieces of graham cracker on the bottom of the air fryer oven. Top each with one of the marshmallows and bake for 6 or 7 minutes, or until the marshmallows have a golden brown center.
3. While cooking, slather each of the remaining graham crackers with 1 teaspoon peanut butter.
4. When baking completes, carefully remove each of the graham crackers, add 1 ounce of dark chocolate on top of the marshmallow, and lightly sprinkle with cinnamon. Top with the remaining peanut butter graham cracker to make the sandwich. Serve immediately.

Apple Juice Piecrust

Servings: 4
Cooking Time: 10 Minutes

Ingredients:

- 1¼ cups unbleached flour
- ¼ cup margarine
- ¼ cup apple juice
- Pinch of grated nutmeg
- Salt to taste

Directions:

1. Preheat the toaster oven to 350° F.
2. Cut together the flour and margarine with a knife or pastry cutter until the mixture is crumbly. Add the apple juice, nutmeg, and salt and cut again to blend. Turn the dough out onto a lightly floured surface and knead for 2 minutes. Roll out into a circle large enough to fit a 9¾-inch pie pan. Pierce in several places to prevent bubbling and press the tines of a fork around the rim to decorate the crust edge.
3. BAKE for 10 minutes, or until lightly browned.

Pear Praline Pie

Servings: 10
Cooking Time: 40 Minutes

Ingredients:

- Pie filling:
- 5 pears, peeled, cored, and sliced, or 3 cups sliced canned pears, well drained
- ½ cup dark brown sugar
- ¼ cup unbleached flour
- ½ teaspoon ground ginger
- 1 teaspoon lemon juice
- Salt to taste
- 1 Apple Juice Piecrust, baked
- Praline topping:
- ½ cup brown sugar
- ½ cup chopped pecans
- ½ cup unbleached flour
- 2 tablespoons margarine

Directions:

1. Preheat the toaster oven to 400° F.
2. Combine the pie filling ingredients in a large bowl, mixing well. Spoon the filling into the piecrust shell.
3. Combine the praline topping ingredients in a small bowl, mixing with a fork until crumbly. Sprinkle evenly on top of the pear mixture.
4. BAKE for 40 minutes, or until the pears are tender and the topping is browned.

Mixed Berry Hand Pies

Servings: 4
Cooking Time: 15 Minutes

Ingredients:

- ¾ cup sugar
- ½ teaspoon ground cinnamon
- 1 tablespoon cornstarch
- 1 cup blueberries
- 1 cup blackberries
- 1 cup raspberries, divided
- 1 teaspoon water
- 1 package refrigerated pie dough (or your own homemade pie dough)
- 1 egg, beaten

Directions:

1. Combine the sugar, cinnamon, and cornstarch in a small saucepan. Add the blueberries, blackberries, and ½ cup of the raspberries. Toss the berries gently to coat them evenly. Add the teaspoon of water to the saucepan and turn the stovetop on to medium-high heat, stirring occasionally. Once the berries break down, release their juice and start to simmer (about 5 minutes), simmer for another couple of minutes and then transfer the mixture to a bowl, stir in the remaining ½ cup of raspberries and let it cool.
2. Preheat the toaster oven to 370°F.
3. Cut the pie dough into four 5-inch circles and four 6-inch circles.
4. Spread the 6-inch circles on a flat surface. Divide the berry filling between all four circles. Brush the perimeter of the dough circles with a little water. Place the 5-inch circles on top of the filling and press the perimeter of the dough circles together to seal. Roll the edges of the bottom circle up over the top circle to make a crust around the filling. Press a fork around the crust to make decorative indentations and to seal the crust shut. Brush the pies with egg wash and sprinkle a little sugar on top. Poke a small hole in the center of each pie with a paring knife to vent the dough.
5. Air-fry two pies at a time. Brush or spray the air fryer oven with oil and place the pies into the air fryer oven. Air-fry for 9 minutes. Turn the pies over and air-fry for another 6 minutes. Serve warm or at room temperature.

Fresh Strawberry Bars

Servings: 16
Cooking Time: 55 Minutes

Ingredients:

- 1 cup unsalted butter, softened
- 2 cups all-purpose flour
- ½ teaspoon table salt
- 1 ⅓ cups sugar
- 2 ½ cups sliced fresh strawberries
- 2 teaspoons fresh lemon juice
- 2 tablespoons cornstarch

Directions:

1. Preheat the toaster oven to 375°F. Line an 8-inch square pan with nonstick aluminum foil.
2. Beat the butter, flour, salt, and 1 cup of the sugar in a large bowl with a handheld mixer at medium speed, until the mixture is combined and resembles crumbles. Place half of the mixture in the prepared pan. Press down evenly to form a crust.
3. Combine the remaining ⅓ cup sugar, the strawberries, lemon juice, and cornstarch in a medium bowl. Spread evenly over the crust. Sprinkle the remaining crumb mixture over the strawberries. Bake for 50 to 55 minutes or until bubbly and light brown. Let cool completely on a wire rack. They are best served at room temperature.

Coconut Rice Cake

Servings: 8
Cooking Time: 30 Minutes

Ingredients:

- 1 cup all-natural coconut water
- 1 cup unsweetened coconut milk
- 1 teaspoon almond extract
- ¼ teaspoon salt
- 4 tablespoons honey
- cooking spray
- ¾ cup raw jasmine rice
- 2 cups sliced or cubed fruit

Directions:

1. In a medium bowl, mix together the coconut water, coconut milk, almond extract, salt, and honey.
2. Spray air fryer oven baking pan with cooking spray and add the rice.
3. Pour liquid mixture over rice.
4. Preheat the toaster oven to 360°F and air-fry for 15 minutes. Stir and air-fry for 15 minutes longer or until rice grains are tender.
5. Allow cake to cool slightly. Run a dull knife around edge of cake, inside the pan. Turn the cake out onto a platter and garnish with fruit.

Scones

Servings: 8
Cooking Time: 20 Minutes

Ingredients:

- Scone mixture:
- 1 cup unbleached flour
- 1 teaspoon baking powder
- 2 ¼ cup brown sugar
- 3 tablespoons vegetable oil
- 4 ¼ cup low-fat buttermilk
- 5 ½ teaspoon vanilla extract
- Topping mixture:
- 1 tablespoon granulated sugar
- 1 tablespoon margarine
- 1 teaspoon ground cinnamon

Directions:

1. Preheat the toaster oven to 425° F.
2. Combine the scone mixture ingredients in a medium bowl, cutting to blend with 2 butter knives or a pastry blender. Add a little more buttermilk, if necessary, so that the dough is moist enough to stay together when pinched.
3. KNEAD the dough on a lightly floured surface for 2 minutes, then place the dough in an oiled or nonstick 9¾-inch round cake pan and pat down to spread out evenly to the edges of the pan. Cut into 8 wedges.
4. Combine the topping mixture in a small bowl, mixing well, and sprinkle evenly on the dough.
5. BAKE for 20 minutes, or until golden brown.

Sour Cream Pound Cake

Servings: 6
Cooking Time: 60 Minutes

Ingredients:

- ¾ cup unsalted butter, plus extra for greasing the baking pan
- 2½ cups all-purpose flour, sifted, plus extra for dusting the baking pan
- 1½ cups granulated sugar
- 4 large eggs
- 2 teaspoons pure vanilla extract
- ½ teaspoon baking soda
- ¾ cup sour cream

Directions:

1. Place the rack in position 1 and preheat the toaster oven to 350°F on BAKE for 5 minutes.
2. Lightly grease and dust a 9-by-5-inch loaf pan.
3. In a large bowl, cream the butter and sugar with an electric hand beater until very light and fluffy, about 4 minutes.
4. Beat in the eggs one at a time, scraping down the sides of the bowl after each addition.
5. Beat in the vanilla.
6. In a medium bowl, stir the flour and baking soda.
7. Fold the flour mixture and sour cream into the butter mixture, alternating two times each, until well combined.
8. Spoon the batter into the loaf pan and bake for 1 hour, or until a toothpick inserted in the center comes out clean.
9. Let cool completely in the pan and serve.

FISH AND SEAFOOD

Crispy Sweet-and-sour Cod Fillets

Servings: 3
Cooking Time: 12 Minutes

Ingredients:

- 1½ cups Plain panko bread crumbs (gluten-free, if a concern)
- 2 tablespoons Regular or low-fat mayonnaise (not fat-free; gluten-free, if a concern)
- ¼ cup Sweet pickle relish
- 3 4- to 5-ounce skinless cod fillets

Directions:

1. Preheat the toaster oven to 400°F.
2. Pour the bread crumbs into a shallow soup plate or a small pie plate. Mix the mayonnaise and relish in a small bowl until well combined. Smear this mixture all over the cod fillets. Set them in the crumbs and turn until evenly coated on all sides, even on the ends.
3. Set the coated cod fillets in the air fryer oven with as much air space between them as possible. They should not touch. Air-fry undisturbed for 12 minutes, or until browned and crisp.
4. Use a nonstick-safe spatula to transfer the cod pieces to a wire rack. Cool for only a minute or two before serving hot.

Roasted Fish With Provençal Crumb Topping

Servings: 3
Cooking Time: 25 Minutes

Ingredients:

- 1 tablespoon olive oil, plus more for greasing
- ⅓ cup finely chopped onion
- 1 clove garlic, minced
- ¾ cup fresh bread crumbs
- 2 tablespoons chopped fresh flat-leaf (Italian) parsley
- 1 teaspoon fresh thyme leaves
- 3 (5-ounce) cod fillets, or other white-fleshed, mild-flavored fish, patted dry (about 1 ¼ inches thick)
- 2 tablespoons dry white wine
- 2 teaspoons fresh lemon juice

Directions:

1. Preheat the toaster oven to 400°F. Lightly grease the baking pan with olive oil.
2. Heat the tablespoon of olive oil in a small skillet over medium-high heat. Add the onion and cook, stirring frequently, for 3 to 4 minutes, or until tender. Add the garlic and cook for 30 seconds. Remove the skillet from the heat. Stir in the bread crumbs, parsley, and thyme.
3. Place the fish in the prepared pan. Drizzle with the wine. Divide the crumb mixture evenly over the top of each fish fillet, and press onto the fillets. Roast for 20 to 25 minutes, or until the top is brown and the fish is opaque and flakes easily when tested with a fork. Sprinkle the lemon juice evenly over the fish.

Maple Balsamic Glazed Salmon

Servings: 4
Cooking Time: 10 Minutes

Ingredients:

- 4 (6-ounce) fillets of salmon
- salt and freshly ground black pepper
- vegetable oil
- ¼ cup pure maple syrup
- 3 tablespoons balsamic vinegar
- 1 teaspoon Dijon mustard

Directions:

1. Preheat the toaster oven to 400°F.
2. Season the salmon well with salt and freshly ground black pepper. Spray or brush the bottom of the air fryer oven with vegetable oil and place the salmon fillets inside. Air-fry the salmon for 5 minutes.
3. While the salmon is air-frying, combine the maple syrup, balsamic vinegar and Dijon mustard in a small saucepan over medium heat and stir to blend well. Let the mixture simmer while the fish is cooking. It should start to thicken slightly, but keep your eye on it so it doesn't burn.
4. Brush the glaze on the salmon fillets and air-fry for an additional 5 minutes. The salmon should feel firm to the touch when finished and the glaze should be nicely browned on top. Brush a little more glaze on top before removing and serving with rice and vegetables, or a nice green salad.

Horseradish-crusted Salmon Fillets

Servings: 3
Cooking Time: 8 Minutes

Ingredients:

- ½ cup Fresh bread crumbs
- 4 tablespoons (¼ cup/½ stick) Butter, melted and cooled
- ¼ cup Jarred prepared white horseradish
- Vegetable oil spray
- 4 6-ounce skin-on salmon fillets

Directions:

1. Preheat the toaster oven to 400°F.
2. Mix the bread crumbs, butter, and horseradish in a bowl until well combined.
3. Take the pan out of the machine. Generously spray the skin side of each fillet. Pick them up one by one with a nonstick-safe spatula and set them in the pan skin side down with as much air space between them as possible. Divide the bread-crumb mixture between the fillets, coating the top of each fillet with an even layer. Generously coat the bread-crumb mixture with vegetable oil spray.
4. Return the pan to the machine and air-fry undisturbed for 8 minutes, or until the topping has lightly browned and the fish is firm but not hard.
5. Use a nonstick-safe spatula to transfer the salmon fillets to serving plates. Cool for 5 minutes before serving. Because of the butter in the topping, it will stay very hot for quite a while. Take care, especially if you're serving these fillets to children.

Pecan-crusted Tilapia

Servings: 4
Cooking Time: 8 Minutes

Ingredients:

- 1 pound skinless, boneless tilapia filets
- ¼ cup butter, melted
- 1 teaspoon minced fresh or dried rosemary
- 1 cup finely chopped pecans
- 1 teaspoon sea salt
- ¼ teaspoon paprika
- 2 tablespoons chopped parsley
- 1 lemon, cut into wedges

Directions:

1. Pat the tilapia filets dry with paper towels.
2. Pour the melted butter over the filets and flip the filets to coat them completely.
3. In a medium bowl, mix together the rosemary, pecans, salt, and paprika.
4. Preheat the toaster oven to 350°F.
5. Place the tilapia filets into the air fryer oven and top with the pecan coating. Air-fry for 6 to 8 minutes. The fish should be firm to the touch and flake easily when fully cooked.
6. Remove the fish from the air fryer oven. Top the fish with chopped parsley and serve with lemon wedges.

Romaine Wraps With Shrimp Filling

Servings: 4
Cooking Time: 8 Minutes

Ingredients:

- Filling:
- 1 6-ounce can tiny shrimp, drained, or 1 cup fresh shrimp, peeled, cooked, and chopped
- ¾ cup canned chickpeas, mashed into 1 tablespoon olive oil
- 2 tablespoons chopped fresh parsley
- 2 tablespoons grated carrot
- 2 tablespoons chopped bell pepper
- 2 tablespoons minced onion
- 2 tablespoons lemon juice
- 1 teaspoon soy sauce
- Freshly ground black pepper to taste
- 4 large romaine lettuce leaves Olive oil
- 3 tablespoons lemon juice
- 1 teaspoon paprika

Directions:

1. Combine the filling ingredients in a bowl, adjusting the seasonings to taste. Spoon equal portions of the filling into the centers of the romaine leaves. Fold the leaves in half, pressing the filling together, overlap the leaf edges, and skewer with toothpicks to fasten. Carefully place the leaves in an oiled or nonstick 8½ × 8½ × 2-inch square baking (cake) pan. Lightly spray or brush the lettuce rolls with olive oil.
2. BROIL for 8 minutes, or until the filling is cooked and the leaves are lightly browned. Remove from the oven, remove the toothpicks, and drizzle with the lemon juice and sprinkle with paprika.

Flounder Fillets

Servings: 4
Cooking Time: 8 Minutes

Ingredients:

- 1 egg white
- 1 tablespoon water
- 1 cup panko breadcrumbs
- 2 tablespoons extra-light virgin olive oil
- 4 4-ounce flounder fillets
- salt and pepper
- oil for misting or cooking spray

Directions:

1. Preheat the toaster oven to 390°F.
2. Beat together egg white and water in shallow dish.
3. In another shallow dish, mix panko crumbs and oil until well combined and crumbly (best done by hand).
4. Season flounder fillets with salt and pepper to taste. Dip each fillet into egg mixture and then roll in panko crumbs, pressing in crumbs so that fish is nicely coated.
5. Spray air fryer oven with nonstick cooking spray and add fillets. Air-fry at 390°F for 3 minutes.
6. Spray fish fillets but do not turn. Cook 5 minutes longer or until golden brown and crispy. Using a spatula, carefully remove fish from air fryer oven and serve.

Coconut-crusted Shrimp

Servings: 4
Cooking Time: 20 Minutes

Ingredients:

- Oil spray (hand-pumped)
- ½ cup all-purpose flour
- 2 large eggs
- ¾ cup unsweetened, shredded coconut
- ½ cup panko bread crumbs
- ¼ teaspoon sea salt
- 1 pound (26 to 30 count) raw extra-large shrimp, peeled and deveined with tails attached

Directions:

1. Preheat the toaster oven to 400°F on AIR FRY for 5 minutes.
2. Place the air-fryer basket in the baking tray and spray it generously with the oil.
3. Place the flour on a plate and set it on your work surface.
4. In a small bowl, whisk the eggs until well beaten and place next to the flour.
5. In a medium bowl, stir the coconut, bread crumbs, and salt, and place next to the eggs.
6. Pat the shrimp dry with paper towels. Working in two batches, dredge the shrimp in the flour, then egg, then coconut mixture, and place them in the basket. Do not crowd the basket.
7. Lightly spray the shrimp with the oil on both sides and in position 2, air fry for 10 minutes, turning halfway through, until golden brown.
8. Repeat with the remaining shrimp, covering the cooked shrimp loosely with foil to keep them warm. Serve.

Tortilla-crusted Tilapia

Servings: 4
Cooking Time: 12 Minutes

Ingredients:

- 4 (5-ounce) tilapia fillets
- ½ teaspoon ground cumin
- Sea salt, for seasoning
- 1 cup tortilla chips, coarsely crushed
- Oil spray (hand-pumped)
- 1 lime, cut into wedges

Directions:

1. Preheat the toaster oven to 375°F on BAKE for 5 minutes.
2. Line the baking tray with parchment paper.
3. Lightly season the fish with the cumin and salt.
4. Press the tortilla chips onto the top of the fish fillets and place them on the baking sheet.
5. Lightly spray the fish with oil.
6. In position 2, bake until golden and just cooked through, about 12 minutes in total.
7. Serve with the lime wedges.

Crispy Smelts

Servings: 3
Cooking Time: 20 Minutes

Ingredients:

- 1 pound Cleaned smelts
- 3 tablespoons Tapioca flour
- Vegetable oil spray
- To taste Coarse sea salt or kosher salt

Directions:

1. Preheat the toaster oven to 400°F.
2. Toss the smelts and tapioca flour in a large bowl until the little fish are evenly coated.
3. Lay the smelts out on a large cutting board. Lightly coat both sides of each fish with vegetable oil spray.
4. When the machine is at temperature, set the smelts close together in the air fryer oven, with a few even overlapping on top. Air-fry undisturbed for 20 minutes, until lightly browned and crisp.
5. Remove from the machine and turn out the fish onto a wire rack. The smelts will most likely come out as one large block, or maybe in a couple of large pieces. Cool for a minute or two, then sprinkle the smelts with salt and break the block(s) into much smaller sections or individual fish to serve.

Stuffed Baked Red Snapper

Servings: 2
Cooking Time: 30 Minutes

Ingredients:

- Stuffing mixture:
- 12 medium shrimp, cooked, peeled, and chopped
- 2 tablespoons multigrain bread crumbs
- 1 teaspoon anchovy paste
- ¼ teaspoon paprika
- Salt to taste
- 2 6-ounce red snapper fillets
- 1 egg
- ½ cup fat-free half-and-half
- 2 tablespoons cooking sherry

Directions:

1. Preheat the toaster oven to 350° F.
2. Combine all the stuffing mixture ingredients in a medium bowl and place a mound of mixture on one end of each fillet. Fold over the other fillet end, skewering the edge with toothpicks.
3. Place the rolled fillets in an oiled or nonstick 8½ × 8½ × 2-inch square baking (cake) pan.
4. Whisk the egg in a small bowl until light in color, then whisk in the half-and-half and sherry. Pour over the fillets. Cover the pan with aluminum foil.
5. BAKE for 30 minutes.

Bacon-wrapped Scallops

Servings: 4
Cooking Time: 8 Minutes

Ingredients:

- 16 large scallops
- 8 bacon strips
- ½ teaspoon black pepper
- ¼ teaspoon smoked paprika

Directions:

1. Pat the scallops dry with a paper towel. Slice each of the bacon strips in half. Wrap 1 bacon strip around 1 scallop and secure with a toothpick. Repeat with the remaining scallops. Season the scallops with pepper and paprika.
2. Preheat the toaster oven to 350°F.
3. Place the bacon-wrapped scallops in the air fryer oven and air-fry for 4 minutes. Cook another 6 to 7 minutes. When the bacon is crispy, the scallops should be cooked through and slightly firm, but not rubbery. Serve immediately.

LUNCH AND DINNER

Spanako Pizza

Servings: 2
Cooking Time: 30 Minutes

Ingredients:

- 8 sheets phyllo dough, thawed and folded in half
- 4 tablespoons olive oil
- 4 tablespoons grated Parmesan cheese
- Topping mixture:
- 1 10-ounce package frozen chopped spinach, thawed and well drained
- 1 plum tomato, finely chopped
- ¼ cup finely chopped onion
- ¼ cup shredded low-fat mozzarella cheese
- 3 tablespoons crumbled feta cheese or part-skim ricotta cheese
- 2 garlic cloves, minced
- Salt and freshly ground black pepper to taste

Directions:

1. Preheat the toaster oven to 375° F.
2. Layer the sheets of phyllo dough in an oiled or nonstick 9¾-inch-diameter baking pan, lightly brushing the top of each sheet with olive oil and folding in the corner edges to fit the pan.
3. Combine the topping mixture ingredients in a bowl and adjust the seasonings to taste. Spread the mixture on top of the phyllo pastry layers and sprinkle with the Parmesan cheese.
4. BAKE for 30 minutes, or until the cheese is melted and the topping is lightly browned. Remove carefully from the pan with a metal spatula.

Classic Tuna Casserole

Servings: 4
Cooking Time: 65 Minutes

Ingredients:

- 1 cup elbow macaroni
- 2 6-ounce cans tuna packed in water, drained well and crumbled
- 1 cup frozen peas 1 6-ounce can button mushrooms, drained
- 1 tablespoon margarine
- Salt and freshly ground black pepper
- 1 cup fat-free half-and-half
- 4 tablespoons unbleached flour
- 1 teaspoon garlic powder
- 1 cup multigrain bread crumbs

Directions:

1. Preheat the toaster oven to 400° F.
2. Combine the macaroni and 3 cups water in a 1-quart 8½ × 8½ × 4-inch ovenproof baking dish, stirring to blend well. Cover with aluminum foil.
3. BAKE, covered, for 35 minutes, or until the macaroni is tender. Remove from the oven and drain well. Return to the baking dish and add the tuna, peas, and mushrooms. Add salt and pepper to taste.
4. Whisk together the half-and-half, flour, and garlic powder in a small bowl until smooth. Add to the macaroni mixture and stir to blend well.
5. BAKE, covered, for 25 minutes. Remove from the oven, sprinkle the top with the bread crumbs, and dot with the margarine. Bake, uncovered, for 10 minutes, or until the top is browned.

French Bread Pizza

Servings: 6
Cooking Time: 8 Minutes

Ingredients:

- 2 tablespoons unsalted butter, melted
- 2 cloves garlic, minced
- ½ teaspoon Italian seasoning
- 1 tablespoon olive oil
- ½ cup chopped onion
- ½ cup chopped green pepper
- 1 cup sliced button or white mushrooms
- 1 (10- to 12-ounce) loaf French or Italian bread, about 12 inches long, split in half lengthwise
- ½ cup pizza sauce
- 6 to 8 slices Canadian bacon or ¼ cup pepperoni slices
- ¼ cup sliced ripe olives, drained
- 1 cup shredded mozzarella cheese
- 3 tablespoons shredded Parmesan cheese

Directions:

1. Preheat the toaster oven to 450°F.
2. Stir the melted butter, garlic, and Italian seasoning in a small bowl; set aside.
3. Heat the oil in a small skillet over medium-high heat. Add the onion and green pepper and sauté, stirring frequently, for 3 minutes. Add the mushrooms and cook, stirring frequently, for 7 to 10 minutes or until the liquid has evaporated. Remove from the heat; set aside.
4. Gently pull a little of the soft bread out of the center of the loaf, making a well. (Take care not to tear the crust.) Brush the garlic butter over the cut sides of the bread.
5. Place both halves of the bread, side by side, cut side up, on a 12 x 12-inch baking pan. Bake for 3 minutes or until heated through. Carefully remove the bread from the oven.
6. Spoon the pizza sauce evenly over the cut sides of the bread. Top evenly with the Canadian bacon, the onion-mushroom mixture, and the olives. Top with the mozzarella and Parmesan cheeses. Return to the oven and bake for 3 to 5 minutes or until the cheese is melted.
7. Cut the French bread pizza crosswise into slices.

Light Quiche Lorraine

Servings: 4
Cooking Time: 35 Minutes

Ingredients:

- Crust:
- 1½ cups bread crumbs
- 1 tablespoon olive oil
- Filling:
- 4 eggs
- ½ cup plain nonfat yogurt
- 2 tablespoons finely chopped scallions
- ¼ cup shredded low-fat mozzarella
- 4 strips lean turkey bacon, broiled, blotted with paper towels, and chopped
- Salt and freshly ground black pepper to taste

Directions:

1. Preheat the toaster oven to 350° F.
2. Combine the bread crumbs, 1 tablespoon water, and the oil in a small bowl and transfer to a pie pan, pressing the mixture flat, starting at the center and working out to the sides. Chill for at least 5 minutes in the refrigerator.
3. Combine the filling ingredients and pour into the chilled bread crumb mixture in the pie pan.
4. BAKE for 40 minutes, or until the center is firm and springy to the touch.

Crab Chowder

Servings: 4
Cooking Time: 40 Minutes

Ingredients:

- 1 6-ounce can lump crabmeat, drained and chopped, or ½ pound fresh crabmeat, cleaned and chopped
- 1 cup skim milk or low-fat soy milk
- 1 cup fat-free half-and-half
- 2 tablespoons unbleached flour
- ¼ cup chopped onion
- ½ cup peeled and diced potato
- 1 carrot, peeled and chopped
- 1 celery stalk, chopped
- 2 garlic cloves, minced
- 2 tablespoons chopped fresh parsley
- ½ teaspoon ground cumin
- 1 teaspoon paprika
- Salt and butcher's pepper to taste

Directions:

1. Preheat the toaster oven to 400° F.
2. Whisk together the milk, half-and-half, and flour in a bowl. Transfer the mixture to a 1-quart 8½ × 8½ × 4-inch ovenproof baking dish. Add all the other ingredients, mixing well. Adjust the seasonings to taste.
3. BAKE, covered, for 40 minutes, or until the vegetables are tender.

Parmesan Artichoke Pizza

Servings: 6
Cooking Time: 15 Minutes

Ingredients:

- CRUST
- ¾ cup warm water (110°F)
- 1 ½ teaspoons active dry yeast
- ¼ teaspoon sugar
- 1 tablespoon olive oil
- 1 teaspoon table salt
- ⅓ cup whole wheat flour
- 1 ½ to 1 ⅔ cups bread flour
- TOPPINGS
- 2 tablespoons olive oil
- 1 teaspoon Italian seasoning
- 1 clove garlic, minced
- ½ cup whole milk ricotta cheese, at room temperature
- ⅔ cup drained, chopped marinated artichokes
- ¼ cup chopped red onion
- 3 tablespoons minced fresh basil
- ½ cup shredded Parmesan cheese
- ⅓ cup shredded mozzarella cheese

Directions:

1. Make the Crust: Place the warm water, yeast, and sugar in a large mixing bowl for a stand mixer. Stir, then let stand for 3 to 5 minutes or until bubbly.
2. Stir in the olive oil, salt, whole wheat flour, and 1 ½ cups bread flour. If the dough is too sticky, stir in an additional 1 to 2 tablespoons bread flour. Beat with the flat (paddle) beater at medium-speed for 5 minutes (or knead by hand for 5 to 7 minutes or until the dough is smooth and elastic). Place in a greased large bowl, turn the dough over, cover with a clean towel, and let stand for 30 to 45 minutes, or until starting to rise.
3. Stir the olive oil, Italian seasoning, and garlic in a small bowl; set aside.
4. Preheat the toaster oven to 450°F. Place a 12-inch pizza pan in the toaster oven while it is preheating.
5. Turn the dough onto a lightly floured surface and pull or roll the dough to make a 12-inch circle. Carefully transfer the crust to the hot pan.
6. Brush the olive oil mixture over the crust. Spread the ricotta evenly over the crust. Top with the artichokes, red onions, fresh basil, Parmesan, and mozzarella. Bake for 13 to 15 minutes, or until the crust is golden brown and the cheese is melted. Let stand for 5 minutes before cutting.

Tomato Bisque

Servings: 4
Cooking Time: 25 Minutes

Ingredients:

- 1 8-ounce can tomato sauce
- 1 7-ounce jar diced pimientos, drained
- 1 tablespoon finely chopped onion
- 2 cups low-fat buttermilk
- 1 cup fat-free half-and-half
- 1 tablespoon low-fat cream cheese
- 1 teaspoon garlic powder
- ½ teaspoon paprika
- ½ teaspoon ground bay leaf
- 1 teaspoon hot sauce (optional)
- Salt and white pepper to taste
- 2 tablespoons minced fresh basil leaves

Directions:

1. Preheat the toaster oven to 350° F.
2. Process all the ingredients except the basil in a blender or food processor until smooth. Pour into a 1-quart 8½ × 8½ × 4-inch ovenproof baking dish. Adjust the seasonings to taste.
3. BAKE, covered, for 25 minutes. Ladle into small soup bowls and garnish each with fresh basil leaves before serving.

Pea Soup

Servings: 6
Cooking Time: 55 Minutes

Ingredients:

- 1 cup dried split peas, ground in a blender to a powderlike consistency
- 3 strips lean turkey bacon, uncooked and chopped
- ¼ cup grated carrots
- ¼ cup grated celery
- 2 tablespoons grated onion
- ½ teaspoon garlic powder
- Salt and freshly ground black pepper to taste
- Garnish:
- 2 tablespoons chopped fresh chives

Directions:

1. Preheat the toaster oven to 400° F.
2. Combine all the ingredients in a 1-quart 8½ × 8½ × 4-inch ovenproof baking dish, mixing well. Adjust the seasonings.
3. BAKE, covered, for 35 minutes. Remove from the oven and stir.
4. BAKE, covered, for another 20 minutes, or until the soup is thickened. Ladle the soup into individual soup bowls and garnish each with chopped fresh chives.

Maple Bacon

Servings: 6
Cooking Time: 16 Minutes

Ingredients:
- 12 slices bacon
- ½ cup packed dark brown sugar
- 2 tablespoons maple syrup
- 1 teaspoon Dijon mustard
- 2 tablespoons red or white wine

Directions:
1. Preheat the toaster oven to 350°F. Line a 12 x 12-inch baking pan with aluminum foil.
2. Place 6 bacon strips on the prepared pan, leaving space between the strips. Bake for 10 minutes or until the bacon is almost crisp. Carefully drain the bacon and return it to the pan.
3. Combine the brown sugar, maple syrup, mustard, and wine in a small bowl. Blend until smooth. Brush the glaze over the bacon. Bake for 8 minutes. Turn the bacon and brush with the glaze. Continue to bake for an additional 6 to 8 minutes, or until golden brown.
4. Repeat with the remaining bacon strips.

Salad Couscous

Servings: 4
Cooking Time: 10 Minutes

Ingredients:

- 1 10-ounce package precooked couscous
- 2 tablespoons olive oil
- Salt and freshly ground black pepper
- ¼ cup chopped fresh tomatoes
- 2 tablespoons chopped fresh basil leaves
- 1 tablespoon sliced almonds
- ½ bell pepper, chopped
- 3 scallions, chopped
- 2 tablespoons lemon juice

Directions:

1. Preheat the toaster oven to 400° F.
2. Mix together the couscous, 2 cups water, and olive oil in a 1-quart 8½ × 8½ × 4-inch ovenproof baking dish. Add salt and pepper to taste. Cover with aluminum foil.
3. BAKE, covered, for 10 minutes, or until the couscous is cooked. Remove from the oven, fluff with a fork and, when cool, add the tomatoes, basil leaves, almonds, pepper, scallions, and lemon juice. Adjust the seasonings to taste. Chill before serving.

Tarragon Beef Ragout

Servings: 6
Cooking Time: 53 Minutes

Ingredients:

- 1 pound lean round steak, cut across the grain of the meat into thin strips, approximately ¼ × 2 inches
- ½ cup dry red wine
- 1 small onion, chopped
- 2 carrots, peeled and thinly sliced
- 3 2 plum tomatoes, chopped
- 1 celery stalk, chopped
- 1 10-ounce package frozen peas
- 3 garlic gloves, minced
- 1 tablespoon Dijon mustard
- ½ teaspoon ground cumin
- ½ teaspoon dried tarragon
- Salt and freshly ground black pepper to taste

Directions:

1. Preheat the toaster oven to 375° F.
2. Combine all the ingredients with ½ cup water in an 8½ × 8½ × 4-inch ovenproof baking dish. Adjust the seasonings. Cover with aluminum foil.
3. BAKE, covered, for 45 minutes, or until the beef, onion, and celery are tender. Remove the cover.
4. BROIL 8 minutes to reduce the liquid and lightly brown the top.

Honey-glazed Ginger Pork Meatballs

Servings: 6
Cooking Time: 20 Minutes

Ingredients:

- 1 ½ pounds ground pork
- 2 tablespoons finely chopped onion
- 3 cloves garlic, minced
- 1 teaspoon minced fresh ginger
- 1 teaspoon sesame oil
- 1 large egg
- 3 tablespoons panko bread crumbs
- Kosher salt and freshly ground black pepper
- HONEY GINGER SAUCE
- 2 tablespoons sesame oil
- 1 tablespoon canola or vegetable oil
- 3 cloves garlic, minced
- 1 ½ tablespoons minced fresh ginger
- 3 tablespoons unseasoned rice wine vinegar
- 1 tablespoon reduced-sodium soy sauce
- 3 tablespoons honey
- 2 to 3 teaspoons garlic chili sauce
- 1 teaspoon cornstarch
- 1 tablespoon cold water
- 2 tablespoons minced fresh cilantro

Directions:

1. Preheat the toaster oven to 375°F. Line a 12 x 12-inch baking pan with nonstick aluminum foil (or if lining the pan with regular foil, spray it with nonstick cooking spray).
2. Combine the pork, onion, garlic, ginger, sesame oil, egg, and panko bread crumbs in a large bowl. Season with salt and pepper. Form into meatballs about 1 ½ inches in diameter. Place the meatballs in the prepared baking pan. Bake for 18 to 20 minutes or until done and a meat thermometer registers 160°F.
3. Make the Honey Ginger Sauce: Combine the sesame oil, canola oil, garlic, and ginger in a medium skillet over medium-high heat. Cook, stirring frequently, for 1 minute. Add the vinegar, soy sauce, honey, and chili sauce and bring to a boil. Whisk the cornstarch with the water in a small bowl. Stir the cornstarch mixture into the sauce and cook, stirring constantly, until thickened. Add the meatballs to the skillet and coat with the sauce. Sprinkle with the cilantro for serving.

POULTRY

Crispy Chicken Parmesan

Servings: 4
Cooking Time: 12 Minutes

Ingredients:

- 4 skinless, boneless chicken breasts, pounded thin to ¼-inch thickness
- 1 teaspoon salt, divided
- ½ teaspoon black pepper, divided
- 1 cup flour
- 2 eggs
- 1 cup panko breadcrumbs
- ½ teaspoon dried oregano
- ½ cup grated Parmesan cheese

Directions:

1. Pat the chicken breasts with a paper towel. Season the chicken with ½ teaspoon of the salt and ¼ teaspoon of the pepper.
2. In a medium bowl, place the flour.
3. In a second bowl, whisk the eggs.
4. In a third bowl, place the breadcrumbs, oregano, cheese, and the remaining ½ teaspoon of salt and ¼ teaspoon of pepper.
5. Dredge the chicken in the flour and shake off the excess. Dip the chicken into the eggs and then into the breadcrumbs. Set the chicken on a plate and repeat with the remaining chicken pieces.
6. Preheat the toaster oven to 360°F.
7. Place the chicken in the air fryer oven and spray liberally with cooking spray. Air-fry for 8 minutes, turn the chicken breasts over, and cook another 4 minutes. When golden brown, check for an internal temperature of 165°F.

Crispy Fried Onion Chicken Breasts

Servings: 2
Cooking Time: 13 Minutes

Ingredients:

- ¼ cup all-purpose flour
- salt and freshly ground black pepper
- 1 egg
- 2 tablespoons Dijon mustard
- 1½ cups crispy fried onions (like French's®)
- ½ teaspoon paprika
- 2 (5-ounce) boneless, skinless chicken breasts
- vegetable or olive oil, in a spray bottle

Directions:

1. Preheat the toaster oven to 380°F.
2. Set up a dredging station with three shallow dishes. Place the flour in the first shallow dish and season well with salt and freshly ground black pepper. Combine the egg and Dijon mustard in a second shallow dish and whisk until smooth. Place the fried onions in a sealed bag and using a rolling pin, crush them into coarse crumbs. Combine these crumbs with the paprika in the third shallow dish.
3. Dredge the chicken breasts in the flour. Shake off any excess flour and dip them into the egg mixture. Let any excess egg drip off. Then coat both sides of the chicken breasts with the crispy onions. Press the crumbs onto the chicken breasts with your hands to make sure they are well adhered.
4. Spray or brush the bottom of the air fryer oven with oil. Transfer the chicken breasts to the air fryer oven and air-fry at 380°F for 13 minutes, turning the chicken over halfway through the cooking time.
5. Serve immediately.

Rotisserie-style Chicken

Servings: 4
Cooking Time: 75 Minutes

Ingredients:

- 1 (3-pound) whole chicken
- 1 teaspoon sea salt
- 1 teaspoon paprika
- 1 teaspoon dried thyme
- 1 teaspoon dried rosemary
- ¼ teaspoon freshly ground black pepper
- 2 tablespoons olive oil

Directions:

1. Preheat the toaster oven to 375°F on CONVECTION BAKE for 5 minutes.
2. Line the baking tray with foil.
3. Pat the chicken dry with paper towels and season all over with the salt, paprika, thyme, rosemary, and pepper. Place the chicken on the baking tray and drizzle with olive oil.
4. In position 1, bake for 1 hour and 15 minutes, until golden brown and the internal temperature of a thigh reads 165°F.
5. Let the chicken rest for 10 minutes and serve.

Golden Seasoned Chicken Wings

Servings: 2
Cooking Time: 40 Minutes

Ingredients:

- Oil spray (hand-pumped)
- ¾ cup all-purpose flour
- 1 teaspoon garlic powder
- 1 teaspoon smoked paprika
- ½ teaspoon sea salt
- ¼ teaspoon freshly ground black pepper
- ¼ teaspoon onion powder
- 2 pounds chicken wing drumettes and flats

Directions:

1. Preheat the toaster oven to 400°F on AIR FRY for 5 minutes.
2. Place the air-fryer basket in the baking tray and spray it generously with the oil.
3. In a medium bowl, stir the flour, garlic powder, paprika, sea salt, pepper, and onion powder until well mixed.
4. Add half the chicken wings to the bowl and toss to coat with the flour.
5. Arrange the wings in the basket and spray both sides lightly with the oil.
6. In position 2, air fry for 20 minutes, turning halfway through, until golden brown and crispy.
7. Repeat with the remaining wings, covering the cooked wings loosely with foil to keep them warm. Serve.

Tender Chicken Meatballs

Servings: 4
Cooking Time: 30 Minutes

Ingredients:

- 1 pound lean ground chicken
- ½ cup bread crumbs
- 1 large egg
- 1 scallion, both white and green parts, finely chopped
- ¼ cup whole milk
- ¼ cup shredded, unsweetened coconut
- 1 tablespoon low-sodium soy sauce
- 1 teaspoon minced garlic
- 1 teaspoon fresh ginger, peeled and grated
- Pinch cayenne powder
- Oil spray (hand-pumped)

Directions:

1. Preheat the toaster oven to 375°F on BAKE for 5 minutes.
2. Line the baking tray with parchment and set aside.
3. In a large bowl, mix the chicken, bread crumbs, egg, scallion, milk, coconut, soy sauce, garlic, ginger, and cayenne until very well combined.
4. Shape the chicken mixture into 1½-inch balls and place them in a single layer on the baking tray. Do not overcrowd them.
5. In position 2, bake for 20 minutes, turning halfway through, until they are cooked through and evenly browned. Serve.

Chicken Souvlaki Gyros

Servings: 4
Cooking Time: 18 Minutes

Ingredients:

- ¼ cup extra-virgin olive oil
- 1 clove garlic, crushed
- 1 tablespoon Italian seasoning
- ½ teaspoon paprika
- ½ lemon, sliced
- ¼ teaspoon salt
- 1 pound boneless, skinless chicken breasts
- 4 whole-grain pita breads
- 1 cup shredded lettuce
- ½ cup chopped tomatoes
- ¼ cup chopped red onion
- ¼ cup cucumber yogurt sauce

Directions:

1. In a large resealable plastic bag, combine the olive oil, garlic, Italian seasoning, paprika, lemon, and salt. Add the chicken to the bag and secure shut. Vigorously shake until all the ingredients are combined. Set in the fridge for 2 hours to marinate.
2. When ready to cook, preheat the toaster oven to 360°F.
3. Liberally spray the air fryer oven with olive oil mist. Remove the chicken from the bag and discard the leftover marinade. Place the chicken into the air fryer oven, allowing enough room between the chicken breasts to flip.
4. Air-fry for 10 minutes, flip, and cook another 8 minutes.
5. Remove the chicken from the air fryer oven when it has cooked (or the internal temperature of the chicken reaches 165°F). Let rest 5 minutes. Then thinly slice the chicken into strips.
6. Assemble the gyros by placing the pita bread on a flat surface and topping with chicken, lettuce, tomatoes, onion, and a drizzle of yogurt sauce.
7. Serve warm.

Roast Chicken

Servings: 6
Cooking Time: 90 Minutes

Ingredients:

- Nonstick cooking spray
- 1 whole (3 ½ -pound) chicken
- Grated zest and juice of 1 lemon
- 1 tablespoon olive oil
- 1 ½ teaspoons kosher salt
- 1 teaspoon garlic powder
- ½ teaspoon dried thyme leaves
- ½ teaspoon freshly ground black pepper

Directions:

1. Preheat the toaster oven to 350°F. Spray a 12 x 12-inch baking pan with nonstick cooking spray.
2. Drizzle the chicken cavity with about half of the lemon juice. Place half of the juiced lemon into the chicken cavity. Truss the chicken using kitchen twine.
3. Rub the chicken evenly with the olive oil.
4. Stir the salt, garlic powder, lemon zest, thyme, and pepper in a small bowl. Using your fingertips, rub the seasonings evenly over the chicken. Place the chicken, breast side up, in the prepared pan. Drizzle with the remaining lemon juice.
5. Roast, uncovered, for 1 ¼ hours to 1 ½ hours, or until a meat thermometer registers 165°F. Let stand for 10 minutes before carving.

Chicken Cordon Bleu

Servings: 4
Cooking Time: 25 Minutes

Ingredients:

- Oil spray (hand-pumped)
- 4 (4-ounce) chicken breasts
- 4 teaspoons Dijon mustard
- 4 slices Gruyère cheese
- 4 slices lean ham
- 1 cup all-purpose flour
- 2 large eggs
- 1 cup bread crumbs
- ½ cup Parmesan cheese

Directions:

1. Preheat the toaster oven to 350°F on AIR FRY for 5 minutes.
2. Place the air-fryer basket in the baking tray and generously spray it with the oil.
3. Place a chicken breast flat on a clean work surface and cut along the length of the breast, almost in half, holding the knife parallel to the counter. Open the breast up like a book and place it between two pieces of plastic wrap. Pound the chicken breast to about ¼-inch thick with a rolling pin or mallet. Repeat with the remaining breasts.
4. Spread the mustard on each breast, place a piece of cheese and ham in the center, and fold the sides of the breast over the cheese and ham. Roll the breast up from the unfolded sides to form a sealed packet. Secure with a toothpick.
5. Repeat with the remaining breasts.
6. Sprinkle the flour on a plate and set it on your work surface.
7. In a small bowl, whisk the eggs until well beaten and place next to the flour.
8. In a medium bowl, stir the bread crumbs and Parmesan and place next to the eggs.
9. Dredge the chicken rolls in the flour, then egg, then the bread crumb mixture, making sure they are completely breaded.
10. Arrange the chicken in the basket and spray lightly all over with the oil.
11. In position 2, air fry for 25 minutes, turning halfway through, until golden brown. Serve.

Apricot Glazed Chicken Thighs

Servings: 2
Cooking Time: 22 Minutes

Ingredients:

- 4 bone-in chicken thighs (about 2 pounds)
- olive oil
- 1 teaspoon salt
- ¼ teaspoon freshly ground black pepper
- ½ teaspoon onion powder
- ¾ cup apricot preserves 1½ tablespoons Dijon mustard
- ½ teaspoon dried thyme
- 1 teaspoon soy sauce
- fresh thyme leaves, for garnish

Directions:

1. Preheat the toaster oven to 380°F.
2. Brush or spray both the air fryer oven and the chicken with the olive oil. Combine the salt, pepper and onion powder and season both sides of the chicken with the spice mixture.
3. Place the seasoned chicken thighs, skin side down in the air fryer oven. Air-fry for 10 minutes.
4. While chicken is cooking, make the glaze by combining the apricot preserves, Dijon mustard, thyme and soy sauce in a small bowl.
5. When the time is up on the air fryer oven, spoon half of the apricot glaze over the chicken thighs and air-fry for 2 minutes. Then flip the chicken thighs over so that the skin side is facing up and air-fry for an additional 8 minutes. Finally, spoon and spread the rest of the glaze evenly over the chicken thighs and air-fry for a final 2 minutes. Transfer the chicken to a serving platter and sprinkle the fresh thyme leaves on top.

Crispy Curry Chicken Tenders

Servings: 4
Cooking Time: 14 Minutes

Ingredients:

- 1 pound boneless skinless chicken tenders
- ¼ cup plain yogurt
- 2 tablespoons thai red curry paste
- 1½ teaspoons salt, divided
- ½ teaspoon pepper
- 1¾ cups panko breadcrumbs
- 1 teaspoon granulated garlic
- 1 teaspoon granulated onion
- Olive oil or avocado oil spray

Directions:

1. Whisk together the yogurt, curry paste, 1 teaspoon of salt, and pepper in a large bowl. Add the chicken tenders and toss to coat. Cover bowl with plastic wrap and marinate in the fridge for 6-8 hours.
2. Combine the panko breadcrumbs, ½ teaspoon salt, garlic, and onion. Remove chicken tenders from the marinade and coat individually in the panko mixture.
3. Preheat the toaster oven to 430°F.
4. Spray both sides of each chicken tender well with olive oil or avocado oil spray, then place into the fry basket.
5. Insert the fry basket at mid position in the preheated oven.
6. Select the Air Fry and Shake functions, adjust time to 14 minutes, and press Start/Pause.
7. Flip chicken tenders halfway through cooking. The Shake Reminder will let you know when.
8. Remove when chicken tenders are golden and crispy.

Honey Lemon Thyme Glazed Cornish Hen

Servings: 2
Cooking Time: 20 Minutes

Ingredients:

- 1 (2-pound) Cornish game hen, split in half
- olive oil
- salt and freshly ground black pepper
- ¼ teaspoon dried thyme
- ¼ cup honey
- 1 tablespoon lemon zest
- juice of 1 lemon
- 1½ teaspoons chopped fresh thyme leaves
- ½ teaspoon soy sauce
- freshly ground black pepper

Directions:

1. Split the game hen in half by cutting down each side of the backbone and then cutting through the breast. Brush or spray both halves of the game hen with the olive oil and then season with the salt, pepper and dried thyme.
2. Preheat the toaster oven to 390°F.
3. Place the game hen, skin side down, into the air fryer oven and air-fry for 5 minutes. Turn the hen halves over and air-fry for 10 minutes.
4. While the hen is cooking, combine the honey, lemon zest and juice, fresh thyme, soy sauce and pepper in a small bowl.
5. When the air fryer oven timer rings, brush the honey glaze onto the game hen and continue to air-fry for another 3 to 5 minutes, just until the hen is nicely glazed, browned and has an internal temperature of 165°F.
6. Let the hen rest for 5 minutes and serve warm.

Orange-glazed Roast Chicken

Servings: 6
Cooking Time: 100 Minutes

Ingredients:

- 1 3-pound whole chicken, rinsed and patted dry with paper towels
- Brushing mixture:
- 2 tablespoons orange juice concentrate
- 1 tablespoon soy sauce
- 1 tablespoon toasted sesame oil
- 1 teaspoon ground ginger
- Salt and freshly ground black pepper to taste

Directions:

1. Preheat the toaster oven to 400° F.
2. Place the chicken, breast side up, in an oiled or nonstick 8½ × 8½ × 2-inch square (cake) pan and brush with the mixture, which has been combined in a small bowl, reserving the remaining mixture. Cover with aluminum foil.
3. BAKE for 1 hour and 20 minutes. Uncover and brush the chicken with remaining mixture.
4. BAKE, uncovered, for 20 minutes, or until the breast is tender when pierced with a fork and golden brown.

SNACKS APPETIZERS AND SIDES

Fried Pickles

Servings: 2
Cooking Time: 15 Minutes

Ingredients:

- 1 egg
- 1 tablespoon milk
- ¼ teaspoon hot sauce
- 2 cups sliced dill pickles, well drained
- ¾ cup breadcrumbs
- oil for misting or cooking spray

Directions:

1. Preheat the toaster oven to 390°F.
2. Beat together egg, milk, and hot sauce in a bowl large enough to hold all the pickles.
3. Add pickles to the egg wash and stir well to coat.
4. Place breadcrumbs in a large plastic bag or container with lid.
5. Drain egg wash from pickles and place them in bag with breadcrumbs. Shake to coat.
6. Pile pickles into air fryer oven and spray with oil.
7. Air-fry for 5 minutes. Spray with oil.
8. Cook 5 more minutes. Shake and spray again. Separate any pickles that have stuck together and mist any spots you've missed.
9. Air-fry for 5 minutes longer or until dark golden brown and crispy.

Classic Cornbread

Servings: 4
Cooking Time: 25 Minutes

Ingredients:

- Oil spray (hand-pumped)
- ¾ cup all-purpose flour
- ¾ cup yellow cornmeal
- ¼ cup granulated sugar
- 2 teaspoons baking powder
- ½ teaspoon sea salt
- ¾ cup buttermilk
- ¼ cup salted butter, melted
- 1 large egg

Directions:

1. Place the rack on position 1 and preheat the toaster oven on BAKE to 400°F for 5 minutes.
2. Lightly oil a 7-inch-round cake pan with the oil spray and set aside.
3. In a medium bowl, stir the flour, cornmeal, sugar, baking powder, and salt until well blended.
4. Make a well in the center and add the buttermilk, melted butter, and egg. Stir until just combined.
5. Spoon the batter into the cake pan and bake for 25 minutes until the cornbread is golden brown and a knife inserted in the center comes out clean. If not ready at 25 minutes, increase the time by 5-minute intervals until baked through. Serve.

Baked Spinach + Artichoke Dip

Servings: 5
Cooking Time: 40 Minutes

Ingredients:

- Nonstick cooking spray
- 2 tablespoons unsalted butter
- ½ medium onion, chopped
- 2 cloves garlic, minced
- 5 ounces frozen, chopped loose-pack spinach (about 1 ¾ cups), thawed and squeezed dry
- 1 (13.75-ounce) can quartered artichoke hearts, drained and chopped
- 1 (8-ounce) package cream cheese, cut into cubes and softened
- ½ cup mayonnaise
- Kosher salt and freshly ground black pepper
- 2 cups shredded Colby Jack or Mexican blend cheese
- ¾ cup shredded Parmesan cheese
- Tortilla chips, pita bread triangles, carrot or celery sticks, broccoli or cauliflower florets, for dipping

Directions:

1. Preheat the toaster oven to 350°F. Spray a 2-quart casserole dish with nonstick cooking spray.
2. Melt the butter in a large skillet over medium-high heat. Add the onion and cook, stirring frequently, until tender, 3 to 5 minutes. Add the garlic and cook, stirring frequently, for 30 seconds. Remove from the heat.
3. Stir in the spinach, artichokes, cream cheese, and mayonnaise. Season with salt and pepper. Blend in the Colby Jack and Parmesan cheeses. Spoon the mixture into the prepared casserole dish. Cover and bake for 20 minutes. Stir the dip and bake, covered, for an additional 10 to 15 minutes, or until hot and melted. Serve with any of the dipping choices.

Simple Holiday Stuffing

Servings: 4
Cooking Time: 120 Minutes

Ingredients:

- 12 ounces hearty white sandwich bread, cut into ½-inch pieces (8 cups)
- 1 onion, chopped fine
- 1 celery rib, chopped fine
- 1 tablespoon unsalted butter, plus 5 tablespoons, melted
- 1 tablespoon minced fresh thyme or 1 teaspoon dried
- 2 teaspoons minced fresh sage or ½ teaspoon dried
- ¾ teaspoon table salt
- ¼ teaspoon pepper
- 1¼ cups chicken broth

Directions:

1. Adjust toaster oven rack to middle position and preheat the toaster oven to 300 degrees. Spread bread into even layer on small rimmed baking sheet and bake until light golden brown, 35 to 45 minutes, tossing halfway through baking. Let bread cool completely on sheet.
2. Increase oven temperature to 375 degrees. Microwave onion, celery, 1 tablespoon butter, thyme, sage, salt, and pepper in covered large bowl, stirring occasionally, until vegetables are softened, 2 to 4 minutes.
3. Stir in broth, then add bread and toss to combine. Let mixture sit for 10 minutes, then toss mixture again until broth is fully absorbed. Transfer bread mixture to 8-inch square baking dish or pan and distribute evenly but do not pack down. (Stuffing can be covered and refrigerated for up to 24 hours; increase covered baking time to 15 minutes.)
4. Drizzle melted butter evenly over top of stuffing. Cover dish tightly with aluminum foil and bake for 10 minutes. Uncover and continue to bake until top is golden brown and crisp, 15 to 25 minutes. Transfer dish to wire rack and let cool for 10 minutes. Serve.

Warm And Salty Edamame

Servings: 4
Cooking Time: 10 Minutes

Ingredients:

- 1 pound Unshelled edamame
- Vegetable oil spray
- ¾ teaspoon Coarse sea salt or kosher salt

Directions:

1. Preheat the toaster oven to 400°F.
2. Place the edamame in a large bowl and lightly coat them with vegetable oil spray. Toss well, spray again, and toss until they are evenly coated.
3. When the machine is at temperature, pour the edamame into the air fryer oven and air-fry, tossing the pan quite often to rearrange the edamame, for 7 minutes, or until warm and aromatic. (Air-fry for 10 minutes if the edamame were frozen and not thawed.)
4. Pour the edamame into a bowl and sprinkle the salt on top. Toss well, then set aside for a couple of minutes before serving with an empty bowl on the side for the pods.

Maple-glazed Acorn Squash

Servings: 2
Cooking Time: 30 Minutes

Ingredients:

- 1 acorn squash (1½ pounds), halved pole to pole, seeded, and cut into 8 wedges
- 1 tablespoon vegetable oil
- 1 teaspoon sugar
- ¼ teaspoon plus pinch table salt, divided
- ¼ teaspoon pepper
- 2 tablespoons maple syrup
- 2 tablespoons unsalted butter
- Pinch cayenne pepper
- 1 teaspoon fresh thyme leaves (optional)

Directions:

1. Adjust toaster oven rack to middle position and preheat the toaster oven to 450 degrees. Toss squash, oil, sugar, ¼ teaspoon salt, and pepper together on small rimmed baking sheet, then arrange cut side down in single layer. Roast until bottoms of squash wedges are deep golden brown, 15 to 20 minutes.
2. Meanwhile, microwave maple syrup, butter, cayenne, and remaining pinch salt in bowl, stirring occasionally, until butter is melted and mixture is slightly thickened, about 90 seconds; cover to keep warm.
3. Remove sheet from oven, and, using spatula, carefully flip squash. Brush with half of glaze and continue to roast until squash is tender and deep golden, 5 to 8 minutes. Carefully flip squash and brush with remaining glaze. Transfer squash to serving platter and sprinkle with thyme, if using. Serve.

Creamy Parmesan Polenta

Servings: 4
Cooking Time: 60 Minutes

Ingredients:

- 2½ cups boiling water, divided, plus extra as needed
- ½ cup coarse-ground cornmeal
- ½ teaspoon table salt
- Pinch baking soda
- 1 ounce Parmesan cheese, grated (½ cup)
- 1 tablespoon unsalted butter

Directions:

1. Adjust toaster oven rack to middle position and preheat the toaster oven to 325 degrees. Combine 2 cups boiling water, cornmeal, salt, and baking soda in greased 8-inch square baking dish or pan. Transfer dish to oven and bake until water is absorbed and polenta is thickened, 35 to 40 minutes, rotating dish halfway through baking.
2. Remove baking dish from oven. Stir in remaining ½ cup boiling water, then stir in Parmesan and butter until polenta is smooth and creamy. Adjust consistency with extra boiling water as needed. Serve.

Turkey Burger Sliders

Servings: 8
Cooking Time: 7 Minutes

Ingredients:

- 1 pound ground turkey
- ¼ teaspoon curry powder
- 1 teaspoon Hoisin sauce
- ½ teaspoon salt
- 8 slider buns
- ½ cup slivered red onions
- ½ cup slivered green or red bell pepper
- ½ cup fresh chopped pineapple (or pineapple tidbits from kids' fruit cups, drained)
- light cream cheese, softened

Directions:

1. Combine turkey, curry powder, Hoisin sauce, and salt and mix together well.
2. Shape turkey mixture into 8 small patties.
3. Place patties in air fryer oven and air-fry at 360°F for 7 minutes, until patties are well done and juices run clear.
4. Place each patty on the bottom half of a slider bun and top with onions, peppers, and pineapple. Spread the remaining bun halves with cream cheese to taste, place on top, and serve.

Crispy Spiced Chickpeas

Servings: 4
Cooking Time: 12 Minutes

Ingredients:

- 1 (15 ounce) can chickpeas, drained, rinsed, and patted dry
- 1 tablespoon olive oil
- ½ teaspoon cumin
- ¼ teaspoon paprika
- ½ teaspoon ground fennel seeds
- ⅛ teaspoon cayenne pepper

Directions:

1. Combine all ingredients in a large bowl and stir to combine.
2. Preheat the toaster oven to 430°F.
3. Place chickpeas on the food tray, then insert the tray at mid position in the preheated oven.
4. Select the Air Fry function, adjust time to 12 minutes, and press Start/Pause.
5. Remove when chickpeas are crispy and golden.

Beef Empanadas

Servings: 8
Cooking Time: 75 Minutes

Ingredients:

- 8 ounces 93 percent lean ground beef
- 3 garlic cloves, minced
- 2 teaspoons chili powder
- 1 teaspoon ground cumin
- 1 teaspoon minced fresh oregano or ¼ teaspoon dried
- 4 ounces Monterey Jack cheese, shredded (1 cup)
- 1 cup mild tomato salsa, drained
- 2 tablespoons chopped fresh cilantro
- 1 package store-bought pie dough
- 1 large egg, lightly beaten

Directions:

1. Microwave beef, garlic, chili powder, cumin, and oregano in bowl, stirring occasionally and breaking up meat with wooden spoon, until beef is no longer pink, about 3 minutes. Transfer beef mixture to fine-mesh strainer set over large bowl and let drain for 10 minutes; discard juices. Return drained beef mixture to now-empty bowl and stir in Monterey Jack, salsa, and cilantro.
2. Adjust toaster oven rack to middle position, select air-fry or convection setting, and preheat the toaster oven to 350 degrees. Line large and small rimmed baking sheets with parchment paper. Roll 1 dough round into 12-inch circle on lightly floured counter. Using 5-inch round biscuit cutter, stamp out 4 rounds; discard dough scraps. Repeat with remaining dough round. Mound beef mixture evenly in center of each stamped round. Fold dough over filling and crimp edges together with fork to seal.
3. Space desired number of empanadas at least 1 inch apart on prepared small sheet; space remaining empanadas evenly on prepared large sheet. Brush all empanadas with egg.
4. Cook small sheet of empanadas until golden brown and crisp, 15 to 25 minutes. Transfer empanadas to wire rack and let cool for 15 minutes before serving.
5. Freeze remaining large sheet of empanadas until firm, about 1 hour. Transfer empanadas to 1-gallon zipper-lock bag and freeze for up to 1 month. Cook frozen empanadas as directed; do not thaw.

Sweet Apple Fries

Servings: 3
Cooking Time: 8 Minutes

Ingredients:

- 2 Medium-size sweet apple(s), such as Gala or Fuji
- 1 Large egg white(s)
- 2 tablespoons Water
- 1½ cups Finely ground gingersnap crumbs (gluten-free, if a concern)
- Vegetable oil spray

Directions:

1. Preheat the toaster oven to 375°F .
2. Peel and core an apple, then cut it into 12 slices . Repeat with more apples as necessary.
3. Whisk the egg white(s) and water in a medium bowl until foamy. Add the apple slices and toss well to coat.
4. Spread the gingersnap crumbs across a dinner plate. Using clean hands, pick up an apple slice, let any excess egg white mixture slip back into the rest, and dredge the slice in the crumbs, coating it lightly but evenly on all sides. Set it aside and continue coating the remaining apple slices.
5. Lightly coat the slices on all sides with vegetable oil spray, then set them curved side down in the air fryer oven in one layer. Air-fry undisturbed for 6 minutes, or until browned and crisp. You may need to air-fry the slices for 2 minutes longer if the temperature is at 360°F.
6. Use kitchen tongs to transfer the slices to a wire rack. Cool for 2 to 3 minutes before serving.

Baked Coconut Shrimp With Curried Chutney

Servings: 8-10
Cooking Time: 11 Minutes

Ingredients:

- 1 cup chutney
- 2 Tablespoons sliced green onion
- 1/2 teaspoon ground curry
- 1/2 teaspoon crushed red pepper
- 2 Tablespoons all-purpose flour
- 1 teaspoon salt
- 1 cup panko breadcrumbs
- 3/4 cup sweetened shredded coconut
- 1 egg white
- 1 pound (16 to 20 count) extra jumbo shrimp
- Cilantro

Directions:

1. In a small bowl, stir chutney, green onion, curry and crushed red pepper until blended. Set aside.
2. Preheat the toaster oven to 450°F. Spray a baking pan with nonstick cooking spray. Set aside.
3. In a large resealable plastic bag, combine flour and salt.
4. Add panko breadcrumbs and coconut to bag. Seal and shake to combine.
5. In a medium bowl, whisk egg white until foamy.
6. Dip one shrimp at a time into egg white.
7. Place shrimp in crumb mixture and press mixture onto shrimp until well coated. Arrange in single layer in prepared baking pan.
8. Bake for 9 to 11 minutes or until crumbs are golden brown. Serve with chutney mixture. Garnish with cilantro.

VEGETABLES AND VEGETARIAN

Street Corn

Servings: 4
Cooking Time: 10 Minutes

Ingredients:

- 1 tablespoon butter
- 4 ears corn
- ⅓ cup plain Greek yogurt
- 2 tablespoons Parmesan cheese
- ½ teaspoon paprika
- ½ teaspoon garlic powder
- ¼ teaspoon salt
- ¼ teaspoon black pepper
- ¼ cup finely chopped cilantro

Directions:

1. Preheat the toaster oven to 400°F.
2. In a medium microwave-safe bowl, melt the butter in the microwave. Lightly brush the outside of the ears of corn with the melted butter.
3. Place the corn into the air fryer oven and air-fry for 5 minutes, flip the corn, and cook another 5 minutes.
4. Meanwhile, in a medium bowl, mix the yogurt, cheese, paprika, garlic powder, salt, and pepper. Set aside.
5. Carefully remove the corn from the air fryer oven and let cool 3 minutes. Brush the outside edges with the yogurt mixture and top with fresh chopped cilantro. Serve immediately.

Chilaquiles

Servings: 4
Cooking Time: 25 Minutes

Ingredients:

- Oil spray (hand-pumped)
- 1¼ cups store-bought salsa
- 1 (15-ounce) can low-sodium navy or black beans, drained and rinsed
- ½ cup corn kernels
- ¼ cup chicken broth
- ¼ sweet onion, chopped
- ½ teaspoon minced garlic
- 25 tortilla chips, broken up into 2-inch pieces
- 1½ cups queso fresco cheese, crumbled
- 1 avocado, chopped
- 1 scallion, white and green parts, chopped

Directions:

1. Place the rack in position 1 and preheat the toaster oven to 400°F on BAKE for 5 minutes.
2. Lightly coat an 8-inch-square baking dish with oil spray and set aside.
3. In a large bowl, stir the salsa, beans, corn, chicken broth, onion, and garlic until well mixed.
4. Add the tortilla chips and stir to combine. It is okay if the tortilla chips break up a little.
5. Transfer the mixture to the baking dish, top with the cheese, and cover tightly with foil.
6. Bake for 20 minutes until the chips are soft, the mixture is bubbly, and then uncover and bake until the cheese is golden and melted, about 5 minutes.
7. Serve topped with the avocado and scallion.

Grits Again

Servings: 2
Cooking Time: 10 Minutes

Ingredients:

- cooked grits
- plain breadcrumbs
- oil for misting or cooking spray
- honey or maple syrup for serving (optional)

Directions:

1. While grits are still warm, spread them into a square or rectangular baking pan, about ½-inch thick. If your grits are thicker than that, scoop some out into another pan.
2. Chill several hours or overnight, until grits are cold and firm.
3. When ready to cook, pour off any water that has collected in pan and cut grits into 2- to 3-inch squares.
4. Dip grits squares in breadcrumbs and place in air fryer oven in single layer, close but not touching.
5. Air-fry at 390°F for 10 minutes, until heated through and crispy brown on the outside.
6. Serve while hot either plain or with a drizzle of honey or maple syrup.

Rosemary Roasted Potatoes With Lemon

Servings: 12
Cooking Time: 4 Minutes

Ingredients:

- 1 pound small red-skinned potatoes, halved or cut into bite-sized chunks
- 1 tablespoon olive oil
- 1 teaspoon finely chopped fresh rosemary
- ¼ teaspoon salt
- freshly ground black pepper
- 1 tablespoon lemon zest

Directions:

1. Preheat the toaster oven to 400°F.
2. Toss the potatoes with the olive oil, rosemary, salt and freshly ground black pepper.
3. Air-fry for 12 minutes (depending on the size of the chunks), tossing the potatoes a few times throughout the cooking process.
4. As soon as the potatoes are tender to a knifepoint, toss them with the lemon zest and more salt if desired.

Blistered Green Beans

Servings: 3
Cooking Time: 10 Minutes

Ingredients:

- ¾ pound Green beans, trimmed on both ends
- 1½ tablespoons Olive oil
- 3 tablespoons Pine nuts
- 1½ tablespoons Balsamic vinegar
- 1½ teaspoons Minced garlic
- ¾ teaspoon Table salt
- ¾ teaspoon Ground black pepper

Directions:

1. Preheat the toaster oven to 400°F.
2. Toss the green beans and oil in a large bowl until all the green beans are glistening.
3. When the machine is at temperature, pile the green beans into the air fryer oven. Air-fry for 10 minutes, tossing often to rearrange the green beans in the air fryer oven, or until blistered and tender.
4. Dump the contents of the air fryer oven into a serving bowl. Add the pine nuts, vinegar, garlic, salt, and pepper. Toss well to coat and combine. Serve warm or at room temperature.

Cauliflower

Servings: 4
Cooking Time: 6 Minutes

Ingredients:

- ½ cup water
- 1 10-ounce package frozen cauliflower (florets)
- 1 teaspoon lemon pepper seasoning

Directions:

1. Pour the water into air fryer oven.
2. Pour the frozen cauliflower into the air fryer oven and sprinkle with lemon pepper seasoning.
3. Air-fry at 390°F for approximately 6 minutes.

Potatoes Au Gratin

Servings: 4
Cooking Time: 40 Minutes

Ingredients:

- Mixture:
- ½ cup fat-free half-and-half
- ¼ cup nonfat plain yogurt
- 2 tablespoons margarine
- 2 tablespoons unbleached flour
- 1 teaspoon garlic powder
- ¼ cup shredded low-fat mozzarella cheese
- 2 tablespoons grated Parmesan cheese
- Salt and butcher's pepper to taste
- 2 cups peeled and diced potatoes
- ½ cup chopped onion
- 1 tablespoon fresh or frozen chives
- ¼ teaspoon paprika

Directions:

1. Preheat the toaster oven to 400° F.
2. Process the mixture ingredients in a food processor or blender until smooth. Pour into a 1-quart 8½ × 8½ × 4-inch ovenproof baking dish.
3. Add the potatoes, onion, chives, and paprika and stir to mix well. Cover the dish with aluminum foil.
4. BAKE, covered, for 40 minutes, or until the potatoes and onion are tender.

Roasted Veggie Kebabs

Servings: 4
Cooking Time: 45 Minutes

Ingredients:

- Brushing mixture:
- 3 tablespoons olive oil
- 1 tablespoon soy sauce
- 1 teaspoon garlic powder
- 1 teaspoon ground cumin
- 2 tablespoons balsamic vinegar
- Salt and freshly ground black pepper to taste
- Cauliflower, zucchini, onion, broccoli, bell pepper, mushrooms, celery, cabbage, beets, and the like, cut into approximately 2 × 2-inch pieces

Directions:

1. Preheat the toaster oven to 400° F.
2. Combine the brushing mixture ingredients in a small bowl, mixing well. Set aside.
3. Skewer the vegetable pieces on 4 9-inch metal skewers and place the skewers lengthwise on a broiling rack with a pan underneath.
4. BAKE for 40 minutes, or until the vegetables are tender, brushing with the mixture every 10 minutes.
5. BROIL for 5 minutes, or until lightly browned.

Molasses Baked Beans

Servings: 4
Cooking Time: 60 Minutes

Ingredients:

- Oil spray (hand-pumped)
- 3 (15-ounce) cans low-sodium canned pinto beans, drained and rinsed
- ½ sweet onion, chopped
- ½ cup low-sodium vegetable broth
- ½ cup tomato paste
- ¼ cup blackstrap molasses
- 1 tablespoon stone-ground mustard
- 1 teaspoon garlic powder

Directions:

1. Place the rack on position 1 and preheat the toaster oven on BAKE to 350°F for 5 minutes.
2. Lightly coat a 1½-quart casserole dish with oil spray.
3. In the dish, combine the beans, onion, broth, tomato paste, molasses, mustard, and garlic powder.
4. Cover the dish with a lid or foil and bake until very tender and the sauce is thick, about 1 hour. Serve.

Asparagus And Cherry Tomato Quiche

Servings: 4
Cooking Time: 50 Minutes

Ingredients:

- 6 asparagus spears, woody ends removed, cut into 1-inch pieces
- 1 premade unbaked pie crust
- 5 large eggs
- ½ cup half-and-half
- ¾ cup shredded Swiss cheese, divided
- Sea salt, for seasoning
- Freshly ground black pepper, for seasoning
- 10 cherry tomatoes, quartered
- 1 scallion, both white and green parts, finely chopped

Directions:

1. Place the rack in position 1 and preheat oven to 350°F on BAKE for 5 minutes.
2. Place a small saucepan three-quarters filled with water on high heat and bring to a boil. Blanch the asparagus until bright green, about 1 minute. Drain and set aside.
3. Line an 8-inch-round pie dish with the pie crust, then trim and flute the edges.
4. In a small bowl, beat the eggs, half-and-half, and ½ cup of the cheese until well blended; season with salt and pepper.
5. Arrange the asparagus, tomatoes, and scallion in the pie crust. Pour in the egg mixture and top with the remaining ¼ cup of cheese.
6. Bake for 45 to 50 minutes until the quiche is puffed and lightly browned, and a knife inserted in the center comes out clean.
7. Serve warm or cold.

Zucchini Boats With Ham And Cheese

Servings: 4
Cooking Time: 12 Minutes

Ingredients:

- 2 6-inch-long zucchini
- 2 ounces Thinly sliced deli ham, any rind removed, meat roughly chopped
- 4 Dry-packed sun-dried tomatoes, chopped
- ⅓ cup Purchased pesto
- ¼ cup Packaged mini croutons
- ¼ cup (about 1 ounce) Shredded semi-firm mozzarella cheese

Directions:

1. Preheat the toaster oven to 375°F .
2. Split the zucchini in half lengthwise and use a flatware spoon or a serrated grapefruit spoon to scoop out the insides of the halves, leaving at least a ¼-inch border all around the zucchini half. (You can save the scooped out insides to add to soups and stews—or even freeze it for a much later use.)
3. Mix the ham, sun-dried tomatoes, pesto, croutons, and half the cheese in a bowl until well combined. Pack this mixture into the zucchini "shells." Top them with the remaining cheese.
4. Set them stuffing side up in the air fryer oven without touching (even a fraction of an inch between them is enough room). Air-fry undisturbed for 12 minutes, or until softened and browned, with the cheese melted on top.
5. Use a nonstick-safe spatula to transfer the zucchini boats stuffing side up on a wire rack. Cool for 5 or 10 minutes before serving.

Vegetable–goat Cheese Flatbreads

Servings: 4
Cooking Time: 17 Minutes

Ingredients:

- 1 (8-inch-wide) rectangular flatbread
- ½ cup store-bought sun-dried tomato pesto
- 12 thin zucchini slices
- ¼ cup mushrooms, thinly sliced
- ¼ red onion, thinly sliced
- 1 tomato, chopped
- ¾ cup goat cheese, crumbled

Directions:

1. Line the baking tray with parchment paper. Place the flatbread on the baking tray and TOAST in position 2 for 5 minutes on medium darkness until lightly crisped. Remove from the oven.
2. Preheat the toaster oven to 400°F on BAKE.
3. Spread the pesto on the flatbread, leaving a ½-inch border along the edge. Scatter the zucchini, mushrooms, onion, and tomato evenly on the flatbread. Top with the goat cheese.
4. Place the baking tray in position 2 and bake for 10 to 12 minutes until crispy and the cheese is melted and lightly browned. Serve.

RECIPES INDEX

Lightning Source UK Ltd.
Milton Keynes UK
UKHW030938270422
402136UK00006B/209

9 781803 19092